ACCORDING TO PLAN

D1387460

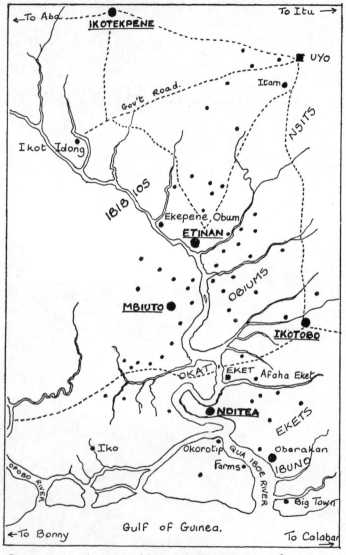

Diagram showing the distribution of Mission Centres and Outstations by 1912.

According to Plan

The Story of Samuel Alexander Bill
Founder of the Qua Iboe Mission, Nigeria

by Jean S. Corbett

Illustrations by Mary Finlay

ISBN 085479 721 1

Printed in Great Britian by Wright's (Sandbach) Ltd., Cheshire

Cover design by Catherine Cheetham

Contents

Foreword

Having had the immense privilege of visiting the territory, and of ministering to the Qua Iboe Church, some 75 years after Samuel Bill set foot upon Nigerian soil, I am delighted that the epic story of his life and work is being put into print for the benefit of the Christian public at large.

The value of Samuel Bill's labours needs only to be known to be appreciated. The foundation he painstakingly laid now bears a superstructure of considerable significance. Despite the ravages of a civil war, that did its utmost to demoralize and sever the church's members into opposite and hostile camps, it stands erect and united as a pillar and buttress of truth, and a fellowship of the Holy Spirit. It is not every kind of supposedly Christian work that has proven its divine qualities through such testing fires.

I heartily commend this beautifully written biography to Christians everywhere. It bears the marks of integrity as it restates the facts relating to the harsh struggle, and persevering toil, of a man of God who was utterly dedicated to his Master's will. There is not a dull chapter. Moreover, apart from the purely historical facts, which exemplify the calling and transformation of a people from paganism until they become trophies of divine grace, and members of the Body of Christ, the pages of this book are spiritually enriching and faith confirming.

Jean Corbett has that rare quality of using words which accurately elucidate the events she describes. Her words never blur the issue. There is a transparency about the record which consistently represents the realities of the situation, without such embellishments as might cloud a single fact. And in this case, the facts are all that matter. Samuel Bill, as well as the emerging church, and the Mission which was, and continues to be, the Lord's instrument in supplying the needs and supporting those who labour on the field, are all vital characters in the ongoing drama of God's saving action in gathering out His elect and building His *ecclesia* in the Qua Iboe territory.

J. Glyn Owen

Preface

A pile of faded diaries and tattered letters, a high regard for Mr. Bill and a sense of divine compulsion – these are the resources from which this little book has been fashioned. It does not pretend to be a definitive history of the Qua Iboe Mission or Church, therefore many significant events and personalities do not appear in its pages. We know that our friends in Church and Mission will understand, for they too, are part of the Plan.

On the evening of September 14 1887, aboard a steamer bound for Calabar, Samuel Bill took out paper and pen, and began to write his diary. Each day of the three weeks' journey, and his first fortnight in Africa, was faithfully described. Then came a break and, apart from a few personal letters, we have no account of his early experiences in Qua Iboe country.

On July 11 1889, he bethought himself, and made a new beginning by writing: 'It is now one year and nine months since I left off the good and useful work of making a daily record of those hopes and fears, joys and sorrows, and all the other events which go to make up an ordinary mortal's existence. While it would be rash to affirm that it is never too late to begin a good work, I might say, without fear of contradiction, that a good work is better begun late than left undone altogether. In this spirit I shall begin again. The best way to redeem the 21 months which are lost in this record will be to carefully collect, and safely store, that of those to come. May this resolution be faithfully and steadily adhered to.'

Meticulous records of over fifty years of missionary service leave us in no doubt about the outcome. During his wife's long absences through ill-health, Mr. Bill's diaries took the form of letters, which she treasured and preserved in neat bundles. Correspondence from the Victorian era is liable to sound ponderous and sentimental in modern ears, but not that of Samuel and Grace Bill. Gracie was a gifted writer with a vivid imagination. Her husband's letters were essentially practical, spiced here and there with shrewd observations, kindly humour and pithy Ulsterisms. He would have regarded with dismay any attempt to eulogise his achievements, so we have tried to present him as he was – an 'ordinary mortal', whom God in His sovereignty chose and equipped to implement His Plan.

Ten years have elapsed since the publication of this biography and it is being re-printed at the request of the Qua Iboe Church, to mark its centenary in 1987. During the intervening decade, the name of the Mission has been changed to *Qua Iboe Fellowship,* and we note that *Ibeno* is now the preferred spelling for the birthplace of the Qua Iboe Church. However, in order to preserve the authenticity of quotations, it has been decided to retain the original name and spelling. Our thanks are due to many friends in Nigeria and elsewhere who gave the first edition such a warm welcome and we pray that its re-issue may bring fresh inspiration and challenge to a new generation of the growing Qua Iboe family.

Jean S. Corbett.

CHAPTER ONE

The Unfolding Plan

'I know the plans I have for you, says the Lord.'
Jeremiah 29:11.

It was the month of June in the year 1887. Meal-time
had ended at Harley Missionary Training College, London, when the principal rose to address his students
who were still seated around the big dining-table. Dr.
Grattan Guinness was an impressive figure, with flowing, silvery hair and aristocratic features. A widely-
travelled evangelist, expositor and missionary statesman,
he had correspondents in many countries, but never before had he received a letter like the one now held in his
hand, bearing the postmark – 'Niger Coast Protectorate.'

'Gentlemen,' he said, 'I have here a remarkable letter.
It has been written by a trader at the request of West
African chiefs. They want a white man to live among
their people and teach them about God. The Scottish
Mission at Calabar has lost so many workers, through
illness and death, that it is unable to answer this call
and has sent it on to me.'

Throwing the travel-stained envelope on the table he
looked round the serious young faces and issued a
formidable challenge.

'It's a treacherous, fever-ridden climate, and canni-
balism is not unknown in the area. You would have no
Mission behind you, but will one of you young men offer
to go?'

As the students dispersed to their various duties in speculative mood, one of their number was strangely silent. No one noticed the gleam in his intensely blue eyes. No one sensed his quickened pulse, or the urgent question burning in his mind. Was this the guidance for which he had prayed so long and earnestly?

Samuel Alexander Bill had come from his native Belfast the previous year to prepare for missionary service in Africa. But Africa was a big continent, and he was nearing the end of training with no further light regarding his eventual destination. World-wide needs were vividly presented in the college, and one student after another discovered his place in the missionary programme. It would have been easy to offer to the Congo Balolo Mission which was associated with Harley. In it he would have had the support of congenial fellow-workers and a reliable home base. But, somehow, there was no assurance that this was God's plan for him.

Today was different. As he listened it seemed as if that letter had been directed to him alone. However, Sam Bill was a canny Ulster Scot, not given to impulsive reactions; before consulting anyone else he must face many issues on his knees before his God.

The first person to consider must be his mother. She had grown up in the atmosphere of the '59 Revival, and its influence permeated her whole life. About the house she sang the familiar hymns and psalms of those halcyon days, and the children never tired of her stories of the power of God in the lives of men. At her knee they learned the Scriptures and many a memorable quotation from the saintly Samuel Rutherford, whose writings took their place beside her well-worn Bible.

Like the mother of yet another Samuel, she had dedicated her son before birth, to the service of God.

It was a commitment from which he had no wish to escape, but he realised something of what their separation might mean to her in coming days. There were no luxuries in the Bill household. Sam had been apprenticed to his father's building firm, and it was a proud day when he took home his first pay, changed into small coins to make it appear bigger, and poured the lot into his mother's lap. Living by faith in Africa would make it hard to give the help she needed, but he knew without being told, that she would be behind him in loving prayer wherever God might lead.

He thought of Bob McCall, the earnest young Sunday School teacher who had led him to the Saviour – an allegiance later confirmed under the powerful preaching of D. L. Moody. Bob would say, 'Sam, never disobey God. It's safe to follow Him anywhere.'

Then there was Archie Bailie, his special friend. Together they had strolled the country lanes on the outskirts of the city, studying the stars and sharing their hopes and dreams. Together they had braced their muscles and tested their endurance, swimming the broad estuary where the Connswater emptied into Belfast Lough. Together they had ventured into Christian service helping in one of the many mission halls which had mushroomed around Belfast, following the Moody and Sankey campaign. Together they had met every Saturday evening, in a little room of Mountpottinger Y.M.C.A., to pray for God's direction and blessing on their lives. Archie was hoping to begin training at Harley College in September. Sam fervently wished he had been with him to hear that letter today.

His thoughts turned naturally from Archie to John McKitterick, a former member of the Bible Class, which both boys attended, in Ballymacarret Presbyterian Church. If the Bills had not moved house, and joined this church, Sam might never have met John, then home on his first furlough from the Congo. It was his account of missionary life that fired the imagination of the teenagers, and drew them to his home to ask more questions about Africa, and the preparation needed for going there. Now that he remembered, Mr. McKitterick had told them about calling at Calabar en route for Congo, and of the urgent need for workers there also. Wouldn't he be surprised at this turn of events!

Dr. Rodgers of Whiteabbey was another person who had a decisive influence on Sam and Archie. This notable preacher had given an illustrated lecture entitled 'Glimpses of the Map of the World' in Ballymacarret Church. It was a foregone conclusion that the friends would attend. On the way home, Sam made an announcement:

'Archie, my mind's made up. I'm going to apply to that college in London that Mr. McKitterick told us about. I believe God wants me to be a missionary.'

Then came training at Harley College. These months had taught him many lessons about himself, about God's Word, about the missionary task, and about living and working with other people. Above all, he had been learning to look to God alone for the supply of daily needs. He owed a lot to the wise counsel of Dr. Guinness and his capable, motherly wife. They would be glad to see his dilemma resolved.

And now the letter. As he thought of it, all the stories he had heard about the intrepid Mary Slessor rose up before him. This call was for someone to penetrate further into that uncharted and mysterious maze of creeks, rivers and malarial swamps then dubbed 'the white man's grave', to reach people of whom little was known except the name of their tribe – IBUNO. It was a daunting prospect, but not so daunting as the fear of disobeying God's call. For, piece by piece, the Plan was unfolding. All the influences, events and circumstances in his life had been working together for a purpose – and that purpose was good.

So it was, that Sam Bill presented himself before the principal's desk.

'Dr. Guinness,' he began diffidently, 'you asked if any of us would answer the call in that letter. I'm here to say that, God helping me, I will.'

The young volunteer did not have to wait long for confirmation. According to custom, a letter was circulated at the end of term briefing the friends who prayed for Harley College and its students. Mention was made of the unusual appeal for a missionary, and the response of the young Ulsterman. By return post came a cheque for £100 to cover his passage to West Africa. Sam never knew the name of the lady who sent that gift, but he never forgot her.

Satisfied by this seal on Sam's offer, Dr. and Mrs. Guinness proceeded to purchase his ticket, and a basic tropical outfit. They could accept no long-term responsibility, but at least 'Harley' would see him on his way. Then, one day in August, they received a surprising message– 'Postponing my sailing till the next boat. Have just found my "Rebecca"'.

The principal and his wife were astounded. Of all their students Sam Bill seemed the least likely to be swept off his feet by a whirlwind romance. To give him his due, he was only postponing departure for three weeks. In the circumstances that spoke volumes for his dedication. But they would have to find out more about this girl. From bitter experience they knew she could make or break his missionary career.

Before returning to Belfast, Sam had gone visiting with his sister and met a gentle English girl with dreamy eyes, finely-cut features, an intelligent mind and a resolution of spirit that matched his own. It was a case of love at first sight, perfectly timed by the Lord who knew his need of a true help meet. Before he sailed on September 14 1887, their engagement had been announced, and Grace Kerr was enrolled as a student at Doric Lodge, the women's section of Harley College.

If it was painful to part from his mother and the friends in Belfast, it was even harder to say goodbye to Gracie, so soon after having found her. Following the hectic rush of preparation, the excitement of farewell meetings and the thrill of a brief courtship, the voyage brought a predictable reaction. Nevertheless the first entries in Samuel Bill's diary foreshadowed the honesty, faith and optimism which were to characterise the rest of his life.

'Left Liverpool today for Calabar. Afternoon cold and wet. Steamer late starting. Feel rather lonely just now. However, all will soon be well. . . .'

The second evening he continued: 'Got up this morning after a sleepless night. Could not sleep for thinking of the past, and those I have left behind; and the future, with all its possibilities of success or failure, of happiness or sorrow – specially of Grace, and how long it might be before we meet again. Found great comfort in the night by committing all those I love to my Heavenly Father, and in remembering that all our steps are ordered by Him in unerring wisdom, and infinite love.'

There was no congenial company on board ship and the young traveller was thankful to have a cabin to himself. Sunday was the hardest day with—

'No churches or meeting houses – and, worst of all, none who know or love the Lord, with whom to have fellowship. However,' he reasoned, 'the way to the throne of grace is always open, and One is there whose delight it is to listen to the breathings of His children. . . . One thing I must write, if this is to be a true record of this day's thoughts, and that is how much my mind is filled with her I have left behind. The union is strong. How

16

strong God knows. And the separation is very hard to bear. Oh, may God bless her richly today with every blessing which she needs; with grace to serve Him at home, and with patience to wait for that time when it may please Him to bring us together again. O Lord, Thou who seest this record, Thou knowest all that is before us: do thou grant, if it be possible, that that time may not be long – and Thou shalt have all the glory.'

At sunrise on September 26, Sam caught his first glimpse of Africa, and his spirits began to rise. He got into argument with some traders about the way nationals should be treated by white men. Burning with indignation he wrote in his diary: 'I am vexed to hear how they speak of the black man. If they could, they would deny that we spring from the same stock.'

At the same time he found opportunities to witness to needy fellow passengers, including one who said he was an agnostic. 'Did not attempt to argue with him, but simply told him the story of my own conversion and that what was to him a myth or an uncertainty was the greatest reality, in fact the moving power of my life.'

A few days later the diary continued: 'Had another talk today with my agnostic friend. Wonder if I shall ever have the pleasure of seeing him converted?'

On the evening before landing, Sam Bill's thoughts were in a turmoil: 'October 5. Nearing my new home,' he recorded. 'Can't help wondering what it will bring! Feel rather downcast and helpless as I draw near the place in which, it is probable, I shall have a hard struggle to obtain a footing. However, He who is with me is more than all they who can be against me. I feel that in His love I can repose, on His wisdom I can depend, and through His power and goodness I shall lack no good thing. I need grace to depend entirely on Him, that I may be faithful in the great work to which He has called me. If I am straitened it must be in

17

myself. Oh for appropriating faith; and then all the fullness of Christ will be mine!'

Next day at sundown the little ship steamed up the Calabar river. As she dropped anchor, numerous canoes paddled out in the dark to meet her. In one of these was Foster, an ex-student of Harley College, come to welcome the newcomer, and initiate him into African ways before the lone Qua Iboe venture. As the canoe pulled in to the riverbank, Sam was puzzled by a peculiar high-pitched sound – like the wind whistling through telegraph wires in a quiet Irish lane, only twice as loud.

'What's the queer noise?' he asked his companion.

'Crickets,' came the unexpected reply. 'Soon you'll never notice them, but they'll be there from dusk till dawn, every night of the year.'

Humid heat wrapped them about as they climbed a steep, slippery slope to the mission house, led by a small, curly-headed lantern-bearer. Fireflies darted through the lush undergrowth. The experienced missionary kept a sharp look-out for snakes, while the younger man absorbed new sights and sounds and smells – strange, yet oddly familiar. Samuel Bill and Africa had met – in the Plan of God.

CHAPTER TWO

Laying the Foundation

'*According to the grace of God which was given unto me . . . I laid a foundation.*' *1 Cor. 3:10.*

'Etubom!'

Sam Bill looked round. He was getting used to the name – literally captain or master of the ship, given by the Efik-speaking Ibunos to all white men.

There before him stood the three children of Williams, an English-speaking African trader, who was one of his new neighbours.

Balanced skilfully on the head of the first little girl was an enamel dish.

'Palm oil chop cooked with snails,' she explained proudly as she handed it to him.

The second child carried two pillows, and the third a couple of bolsters, made by their mother from local cotton.

'Her kindness never flags,' was Sam's comment in his diary that night. 'She is continually doing something for me. May God reward her.'

Early in the New Year, Sam had left Calabar in the small steamer, which plied its way, every three weeks, along the muddy coastline and up the clear waters of the Qua Iboe river to the trading centre at Eket. It did not usually stop at the fishing village of Ibuno, but the rule was broken to deposit the young Ulsterman and his few belongings among the people awaiting his arrival. He liked the place immediately.

'It is within sight of the sea,' he wrote. 'You can sit on the verandah of the house, and look across the Atlantic in one direction, and up the river in the other, while the roar of the water is continually heard as it breaks on the bar of the river about four miles off. The house is not finished.'

The house, begun in anticipation of his coming, was far from finished. It was raised from the ground on poles like the white men's houses at Calabar, but only an outer shell was up, and there was no floor. The roof of palm leaf mats let the rain through like a sieve. Running an expert eye over it, Sam knew his first job must be to make it weather-proof, so with the help of a few boys, he began to cut timber from the surrounding palm forest to strengthen the walls. Floor-boards had to come from the United Africa Company's stores at Calabar. The agent there proved to be another friend in need.

'How many pieces of scantling, and sheets of iron would it take to put a decent roof on your house?' he enquired.

Sam did a quick calculation.

'But I'll have to wait a while to get the money for that,' he hastened to explain.

'Oh no you won't,' corrected the Englishman. 'I'm giving it to you for a present.'

Mr. Hagoo may not have understood what prompted the young pioneer to choose a life of privation, but he admired his pluck and wanted to get a sound roof over his head before the onset of torrential rains.

While work went on, Sam occupied a mud house reserved for the use of traders. He got little sleep and would have fared badly had it not been for the Williams's, about whose kindness he wrote to friends at home who watched anxiously for his three-weekly bulletins.

'When they saw I had trouble getting my food cooked they kept sending for me at every meal-time, asking me to have it with them. As they did not seem pleased if I did not go, I consented to go twice a day for a while, and to make my own breakfast as best I could. Thus you see how the Lord raised up help in the hour of need.'

'Mrs. Williams also washed my clothes, and she is now teaching a boy to bake bread for me. For the last few weeks I have not been well – gum-boil, fever, and headache with loss of appetite. Add to this sleeping at night with a gun beside me to beat off the rats, so that I don't feel up to writing all the friends I promised.'

During the first four months, almost every week brought a fresh attack of the malaria which was rampant in the area. Ill-health, privation and loneliness might have daunted a less determined pioneer, but Sam was quick to reassure his correspondents:

'You can have no idea how busy I am at present. . . . I see by your last letter you are alarmed about my first fever, but you need not be – I have got over it and many more of the same kind. The people here tell me it is much better to have slight fevers often, than to have one very high fever.'

'As to food, you need not fear. I have not wanted for anything needful. Just now, as my first supplies are running down, I have received the invoice of another supply sent by Mrs. Guinness, and it is lying at Calabar waiting to be brought up-river. Then, Mr. Williams and others are always sending me presents of fish, and other things. I have never asked for anything – and yet it is thus that our Heavenly Father supplies my need.'

Although Sam was sure of his call and sure of his God, he was by no means sure of himself. By nature he was energetic, and liked to get things done. Now he had to readjust to a different tempo of life, and he found it difficult to be patient. Then there was the all-important matter of maintaining his personal devotion, without the stimulus of Christian fellowship.

The pages of his diary reflect some of these spiritual struggles: 'I feel deeply my own need of more love to Jesus. When I think of all He has done for me, and how little love stirs my heart for Him, then I know I am not worthy of the name of "Christian". O, my God, help me to examine myself – and that with an impartial eye.'

'Show me myself, but O, show me Jesus. If He does not save me I am lost. Give me evidence that my faith is of a saving kind, by enabling me to overcome all sin . . . my quick temper . . . and also by setting my heart aflame with love to Thee. How parched and dry my spiritual life is at this time. O my Lord, I want to love Thee supremely. Let no other idol have any of my affection, and help me to be faithful to Jesus, testifying to all I meet of His love and grace.'

'O God, make Thy name great in this place,' was his longing. 'Let the name of Jesus be highly esteemed by these people. Do Thou fire my heart with zeal for Thy glory, and grant that my only satisfaction may be to do Thy will and to spend, and be spent in Thy service.'

As he began to understand what the people were saying, and to speak a little Efik in return, Samuel Bill was learning a lot about the Ibunos and the motives which had prompted their momentous invitation. They were gentle, peaceable folk who, under persecution, had broken away from a larger tribe in the west, and settled in uninhabited land near the sea. For years they had acted as middlemen between the Europeans at Calabar, and the peoples of the interior, bartering cloth, gin and

" ...... offerings of eggs, palm wine or fowl..... "

household utensils for palm oil, nuts and timber. They were expert fishermen, using traps or nets made from tough palm creeper, each of which occupied about twelve feet of river bank. These sites passed from generation to generation of the same family, and were never sold – though in hard times they might be mortgaged. Constantly worked by one individual, with additional help for pulling up the stakes, a net could catch a great quantity of fish, which was then dried, salted and sold up-country.

Like all their surrounding tribes, the Ibunos were animists, with a vague belief in a Supreme Being, too remote to be concerned in the affairs of mere men. They had an intense awareness of spirits, who must be continually propitiated by offerings of eggs, palm wine, fowl, or goats. When they made human sacrifice it was through no desire to shed blood, but as a last resort to prevent calamity befalling their people. A great fear of witchcraft and multiple births led to the killing of suspect witches and twin children, one of whom was believed to be the progeny of an evil spirit.

Twelve years previously the Ibunos had been attacked by a neighbouring chief, bent on annexing their markets and fishing rights. Hundreds of armed men in fifty war canoes mounted with breech-loading cannon, invaded the peaceful community – burning, looting, killing, enslaving, and driving the survivors up-river into hiding.

Years later the refugees ventured back, to find their homes in ashes and farms overgrown. Gathering on the site of the old Efe, or drinking house, the headmen discussed their situation. The river still abounded in fish and the forest in creeper from which to weave new nets. They wanted to resettle among the spirits of their forefathers, but would the ancient rites and sacrificces be able to protect them in the event of another invasion? That was the important question.

'Let us ask for a white teacher,' suggested one chief, who had met some missionaries on his trading trips to Calabar. 'If a white man lived among us our enemies might fear to attack.'

'And our children might learn book, and become better traders,' added another.

After much palaver the people agreed. In due course the fateful letter was written, carried to the Scottish missionaries and forwarded to London.

Sam Bill was not disturbed to discover that the invitation had not been prompted wholly by thirst for the Gospel. God had used that letter to direct his steps to Ibuno. There must be a work for him to do among these friendly fisher-folk, for whom he had a growing respect and affection.

Ibuno houses were rectangular and made of mud and wattle, with mat roofs. They were sited in groups, to accommodate the headman and his various wives and children, round an open yard or compound. Some of these families welcomed the missionary's visits and gave him a good hearing. He was grateful that he did not have to start from scratch with an unwritten language, for Ibuno Efik differed only slightly from the Calabar Efik, into which the Bible had already been translated. So, accompanied by one of the boys as interpreter, and armed with a small manual of English/Efik texts, he began to explain, as simply as possible, the story of God's love and redeeming grace. The young people loved to sing. Sam, always fond of music, was delighted to find they could learn and enjoy his favourite hymns and metrical psalms.

From the outset he had been gathering a few boys for reading and Scripture lessons on the verandah of his house. Pupils would attend this very irregular school for a few days, and then disappear for weeks on end to help on the farms, or accompany their parents to more productive fishing grounds – not to mention the numerous occasions when the teacher was too ill to teach them. As time went on, however, Sam felt the need for a separate building to serve as church and school. Realising the importance of doing things according to local custom, he met the chiefs to explain what he wanted – and they agreed to summon the people to work.

The procedure fascinated the young builder. First, a law was enacted that a man must go and cut stout stakes, about ten feet tall. Then, another law was made, for people to point the stakes with their sharp machetes.

These stakes were driven into the ground to form a rectangle about forty-eight feet long, by eighteen feet wide. A third group was directed to get bamboos, split them, and stick them in between the stakes, about three feet apart. More sticks were woven through these, and then the women plastered the framework with smooth clay. The roof was provided by the children, who sewed leathery palm leaves into mats for thatching.

It took a long time to get the job finished, and Sam's patience was sorely tried, but it was with a sense of real achievement that he finally dedicated that first simple structure to the worship of God. From then on, two services were held there every Sunday, and on week-days it served as a school for anything from ten to thirty pupils.

Having learned how to construct a mud building, Sam proceeded to organise his three helpers to erect houses for themselves beside his own. Together they cut and prepared the timber and bamboo, learning to know and understand each other in the process.

'Now we are ready to mud the walls,' he announced one day.

The horrified expression on the boys' faces told him he had made a serious mistake.

'Etubom, that is women's work,' they protested indignantly. 'No man must mud walls.'

So that was that! Some ingenuity would be required to solve this problem.

One of the friendliest chiefs, and a frequent visitor, was Chief Egbo-Egbo. He too was erecting a new house. He greatly admired the doors Etubom had made, but had no carpenter to do a similar job.

'If I make doors for you, will you send your wives to mud the boys' houses?' ventured the resourceful Sam.

Egbo-Egbo was delighted, and before long his twelve wives were hard at work, while the missionary got going with hammer and chisel. The carpentry took less time than the mudding, and the women thought their husband had made a bad bargain, but the two men were satisfied, and became firm friends! With God-given instinct Samuel Bill was laying a foundation of mutual respect, trust, and good humour that would stand the test of time.

CHAPTER THREE

Chief Corner Stone

'Jesus Christ Himself being the chief corner stone.'
Eph. 2:20.

It was a great day for Sam when Archie Bailie arrived in Africa. Many letters had passed between the two while Archie studied at Harley College, but neither took it for granted that because one had gone to Qua Iboe, the other would necessarily follow.

After a year at Ibuno, Sam confessed: 'Sometimes I feel I have been a long, long time away from home. I am very glad to hear A. Bailie is coming out. I am tired of being alone and he will be such a help in the work.'

Now that Archie had arrived, there seemed no end to the possibilities stretching out before them. With him came a letter from a hitherto unknown friend, asking many questions about Sam's life and work. Replying, the young pioneer gave a typically unromantic account of his day-to-day activities: 'My work consists in house-building, cooking, teaching, preaching, clearing bush off the ground and keeping it clear, also acting as a judge in disputes, and every other imaginable kind of work. There is no fear of a missionary who wants to establish a self-supporting mission thinking long for want of variety. Some of the work which I have to do is not, as you will see, of the most dignified type, but all work done for the Master is ennobled when it is performed in His service and for His sake.'

Christian fellowship was what Sam Bill missed most during his first year at Ibuno. Now, at last, he had someone with whom to pray. Constant callers made privacy difficult at the half-finished house where the missionaries lived so they decided to build a mud hut, deep in the bush, where they could pray without being disturbed. There, day after day, they kept tryst with God, and this was the burden of their prayer – 'O Lord, call out from among these people, a Church of two hundred believers for the glory of Thy Name. Break the powers of darkness that bind them, and open their eyes to see Jesus as their Saviour and Deliverer.'

Both men agreed that life would have been well-spent if they could see that vision fulfilled.

At times it seemed a long way off. The people were friendly, but Sam noted: 'When they hear the Gospel, and what it demands of them, they are inclined to turn against it. However, I look forward to the time, not far distant, when Jesus shall triumph.'

Sunday services were encouraging, with more than a hundred people gathering in the morning, and a core of regular attenders who were listening with close interest. And still there was the challenge of numberless unreached villages flanking the river, as it narrowed northward through the palm forest.

In November 1889 the two men set out to explore. Beyond Ibuno territory they entered the thickly-populated Eket country. Next came the Ibibio tribe, believed to be the largest of the three, extending from the Bonny to the Calabar rivers. Then the Annangs and, beyond their reach by canoe, the great unevangelised Ibo tribe.

Earlier, Sam Bill had summed up his impressions of conditions around Ibuno. 'Dark superstition, polygamy, slavery, rum and gin have been, and are, doing their terrible work. Rum and gin are, I solemnly believe, worse than any of the others. It is a burning shame to England, to her commerce, and above all her Christianity, that her merchants should try to make themselves rich at the expense of these poor people's health and happiness. I can tuly say that drink is their greatest curse, and I speak from what I see from day to day.'

This diagnosis was confirmed, as he stood with Archie on the wharf at Eket and watched the unloading of 3,000 cases of gin and as many barrels of rum. Wherever they set foot the same traffic was in progress – 'degrading and depopulating the tribes, more than all their heathen ordinances. Although we visited towns to which no other white men have been yet, we were painfully conscious of the curse of gin and rum in them all. Many of the poor victims testified – "It is killing many of our people" '.

Usually, the missionaries were well received.

'If you were coming to trade with us we would make you welcome,' said the chiefs in one place. 'Still, we do not object to a teacher. This is a thing of which we have never heard before.'

'If it were not so late, we would tell you some things from God's Word,' responded Sam Bill.

'We would like to hear, and you are able to walk by the light of the moon,' they persuaded.

So, there and then, he preached to them of God, and of Jesus, of sin, and heaven and of hell.

'These are very serious things you tell us,' acknowledged the chiefs. 'We would like to hear more.'

So it was, in town after town. The men returned to Ibuno, burdened by the magnitude of the task, and the depth of the need. 'But,' wrote Archie, 'We have the covenant-keeping Jehovah on our side. It is He Who commands us to go, and we can do all things through Christ Who strengthens us.'

Morning and evening they met with their three houseboys, around the Word of God. Samuel Bill recalled years later: 'It was here that the spiritual part of our work really began. These boys became very much interested in what they heard, and some of them were our first Christians. One of the first was David. After I had been there for some time he came in very great distress about his soul, and asked me to tell him how he could follow God and have his sins put away. You can understand how glad I was . . .'

David Ekong was the son of a principal chief, and grandson of the High Priest of Ekong. At fourteen years of age he had been initiated into the secret order, having proved his courage by handling the gory head of a beheaded slave and tasting the blood. After this grim ordeal he was permitted to assist at sacrifices to the great spirit, Nyena, and was fully expected to succeed to the high priesthood and chieftaincy of his people. But God had a higher destiny for David Ekong. In the interval between the sending of the invitation, and the arrival of Samuel Bill, some Christians from Calabar had preached at Ibuno, and David's interest had been aroused. When the missionary appeared, this intelligent lad was waiting to become his houseboy and interpreter.

If ever a church was blessed in its first convert, it was the Qua Iboe Church in David Ekong. Sam Bill could remember only one set-back in his spiritual growth. Some months after receiving assurance of forgiveness he seemed to lose interest, and the missionary enquired what was wrong. No immediate explanation was forthcoming but in the middle of the following night Sam awoke from sleep to find the lad at his bedside, weeping bitterly.

'Etubom, I have been grieved since you spoke to me today. It is true I have not been walking with God. Is there any way for me to get back to Him?'

By the flickering light of a bush lamp, two heads bent low over an opened Bible. There *was* a way back to God – a true and living Way. The boy must have grasped quickly the secret of abiding in Him, for, long afterwards, his spiritual guide could write, 'From that time, David has gone on from strength to strength.'

The first woman to be baptised was Etia. She had been the wife of a chief, after whose death she was stripped of all possessions. With her little son she returned home to Big Town, only to be forced to flee again before the invading war canoes in 1875. Back home once more, her troubles were far from over. A child of another family died, and Etia was accused of having killed him by witchcraft. To an Ibuno woman in those days only two courses were open; either she must agree to speedy death or try to clear herself by eating a poisonous bean. If the latter proved fatal her guilt would be established. If she survived she was proclaimed innocent. Etia ate the bean and although she suffered agonies, her life was spared.

Soon after this, some of the Calabar Christians arrived to conduct meetings and one of them stayed at the home of Etia and her second husband. Through his preaching she came to see the folly of idolatry, and, at length, decided to burn the wooden idols representing the spirit of her forefathers. Tremblingly she chopped them up for fuel to cook her food. No harm followed the meal, so, gathering courage, she smashed the little saucer treasured by every Ibuno woman as the place where her soul was supposed to dwell. It was a big step of faith for she did not yet know the living God, but He had anticipated her search, and His messenger was already on the way.

By the time Samuel Bill reached Qua Iboe, Etia's second husband was dead. She built a little house near the Mission and attended all the services, deeply convicted by the Holy Spirit.

'My sins are very many,' was her cry. 'How can they be put away?'

For some months she and David Ekong were instructed together in the way of salvation and as Etubom got a better grasp of Efik the enquirers gained a clearer understanding of the truth. Before long, both were witnessing to new life in Christ, and they became the first believers to be baptised in Qua Iboe.

Chief Egbo Egbo was another frequent church attender. As one of the prime movers in asking for a missionary, he went out of his way to be helpful and friendly. There his interest seemed to stop, until one day, at the end of two years, he announced,

'Etubom, I want to follow God.'

Now Sam Bill had become very fond of the genial, generous chief. He longed to see him a true believer, but what about the twelve wives and the gin-trading and slave-dealing?

The seeking man came every day to study the Scriptures, but seemed to make little progress. At last, David Ekong, eager to share his own experience, suggested,

'May I go to Egbo Egbo's house and teach him how he can find peace through the blood of Jesus?'

The missionary wondered how the chief would react to being instructed by a boy.

'Nothing would please me so much,' he assured them.

So, explaining that only the Holy Spirit could open blinded eyes, Sam sent them off together, and prayed for a miracle of enlightenment.

'Well David?' he enquired later.

'Etubom, he go see,' reported the youthful evangelist, with evident satisfaction.

After four days' instruction, he brought his pupil back to the mission house to be questioned. 'I was glad indeed,' wrote Sam Bill, 'to find that he was able, with heart and understanding, to commit himself to Jesus Christ, and to know, by faith, that his sins were taken away by the finished work of Christ. Thus, what we could not help this man to see, it pleased God to reveal through the ministrations of this boy.'

David continued to teach the chief daily, and Etubom observed, 'It is a blessed thing to see this once proud chief, a patriarch of his tribe, sitting meekly at the feet of Jesus and receiving His truth from the mouth of a boy.'

This proved to be a momentous event in the history of the Qua Iboe missionary enterprise. It marked the transformation of an influential leader into a devoted follower of Christ, the emergence of the Church's first evangelist and pastor, and the revelation of the right pattern for the future. The missionary's top priority must be to commit the truth to faithful men, who would be able to teach others also.

CHAPTER FOUR

Built Together

'The Lord: in Whom ye also are builded together...'
Eph. 2:22.

On the same side of the river as Ibuno but nearer the coastline, lay the large creek-settlement of Impanek, or Big Town. From there, every day, John Nwaining paddled his canoe to attend the white man's school. Many a flogging he received from his outraged heathen father, but John had seen a vision, and heard a voice. Nothing could turn him back.

Soon after the arrival of Archie Bailie it was decided to begin a school at Big Town. John and his friends, were anxious for their teacher to live among them, so the missionaries set out one day to explore the territory. Sam Bill described their journey:

'Archie and I went today to find out for certain if there was a path from Big Town, on the creek, to the beach of the Qua Iboe River at the seashore. There is no path, and no possibility of making one. It is all swamp, and full of elephant tracks and droppings. Not a human footprint anywhere!

'Such an experience as today's in surveying the swamp we never had before. It was covered for the most part with dense bush and prickly palm trees. At times we were up to the knees in mud and water. Then we had to crawl on all fours to get through tangled undergrowth. We encountered one snake; but it slid away before I could get a shot at it.

'We are pretty well stocked with thorns, and our shins are black and blue from hitting against tree-trunks. The practical outcome of all this is, that it knocks on the head any idea we may have entertained of Archie's settling at Big Town. This swamp is the home of elephants, wild pigs, leopards, deer, and dangerous snakes.'

There was great disappointment at the decision but, travelling the half hour's journey by canoe from Ibuno, Archie Bailie, with John's help, continued to conduct Sunday services and regular classes. The young believer was full of enthusiasm, and went around the riverine markets, playing his concertina, singing hymns, and preaching the Lord Jesus.

One Wednesday morning about nine o'clock two runners arrived at Ibuno.

'An elephant is doing much damage to the farms at Big Town,' was their message. 'The hunters have hit him and he is angry, but they cannot kill him. Will Etubom please come and shoot him?'

Grabbing his Martini rifle and all the cartridges he could muster, Sam accompanied them to the scene of action – a forest belt bordering a yam and maize plot. The farm was full of men, armed with weapons of all kinds from the snider down to the old flint-lock. Between the plantation and the creek lay a narrow strip of dense bush into which the injured beast had retreated.

'Just a few minutes after I arrived,' wrote Sam Bill 'he made a tremendous charge in my direction – not coming clear out of the bush, but to within about ten yards of the edge. We could see the line of his huge back above the tops of the undergrowth, and hear the peculiar noise he was making, like a most frantic blowing of the nose. The sound of his charge was fear-inspiring to the last degree. Young trees were broken and brushed aside like meadow grass. His speed was such that no man in his track could possibly escape. He was very angry too, for they had been firing at him from the yam plot for fully two hours.

'I entered the bush, not I must confess, without fear, for the disturbing echo of that onrushing charge was still fresh in my ears. Two or three men came with me. I dodged him, putting a bullet in here and there. Once, I got entangled in creepers and fell. I crawled to one side, hoping he could not see me. He came towards me but stopped, thank God, within about ten yards. I got four more shots in – then he made for the creek. I followed, putting many more bullets in his head, as I got the chance. When he reached the water, he fell with his magnificent tusks deeply dug into the mud. The forest giant was dead.'

'Akpa, Akpa' – the cry echoed round the town, to tell the people the marauder had been laid low.

Sam gazed down at the noble beast. It gave him no pleasure to kill, but at least no human life had been lost, and further damage to farms and homes had been averted. The people were overjoyed, and swarmed around, machetes at the ready, to claim share of the spoil. The owner of the plantation called an 'Ekpo' by placing a few palm leaves on the carcase as a prohibition against any interference, till an Ekpo priest decided what was to be done with it. To his chagrin, no one paid the slightest heed, hacking away to take home as much flesh as they could carry.

'He might as well have put salt on it,' was Sam's wry comment.

Without doubt, the power of the Ekpo Secret Society was being undermined. If its activities had been confined to such innocent matters as disposing of a carcase, it might have survived the impact of the Gospel, but no true Christian could condone the cruelties perpetrated in its name. Within a month of arriving in Africa, Sam Bill had written about his first encounter with the cult:

'I went today to see what is called Ekpo. It is a Secret Society, whose members turn out in a very fantastic attire. No part of the body can be seen except the feet and the ankles. With some the ankles – even the skirts – are covered with bells. As they dance along, throwing their quivering bodies into all kinds of shapes, the bells keep tinkling. Some of them wear a huge head-dress, made in the form of the bellows of a concertina, which they can throw up in the air, to a distance of four or five feet.

'The Ekpo has been responsible for great cruelties. Sometimes men, and oftener women, have been flogged to death when they chanced to intercept their paths. Although the presence of the Government has to some extent checked their gross outrages, yet this order still exerts considerable power. When Ekpo is blown, no man would dare to disobey the summons. On the opposite side of the river from my house, during an Ekpo demonstration, some boys were badly cut up and one lad was held while his arm was singed with a burning brand.'

Many of the new believers were suffering for their faith. Several school boys were beaten up, and Chief Egbo Egbo was also assaulted, but persecution did not succeed in shaking his faith. After Christian marriage to his first wife, he had made provision for the support of the other eleven, all of whom became Christians, and most of whom eventually re-married. Slave-trading had been abandoned, and debts to European traders had been paid, but his greatest stumbling-block had been the gin traffic.

'But Etubom,' he reasoned, 'When the white man first brought the stuff, no one liked it. Now everyone wants it more than anything else. Half my income comes from selling it. How can I give that up?'

Sam and Archie had many a discussion and prayer about the problem.

'We do not say you cannot be a Christian unless you stop the trade in spirits,' was their verdict. 'Only God can judge that. But we cannot see our way to baptise you while you still engage in it.'

The chief went away crestfallen, and that night Sam wrote in his diary: 'The stand we have taken will not, humanly speaking, tend to increase the number of our converts; but God will call us to account, not for the number of our church members, but for faithfulness to the light He has given us.'

Two months later Egbo Egbo appeared, beaming from ear to ear. The struggle was over, and so was the gin traffic. Some effort had to be made to compensate for the loss of income, so he decided to start a new palm-oil market farther up-river. It was there that he and his servants were attacked and flogged but, in spite of receiving shameful treatment and spitting in his face, the good man neither retaliated nor ceased to speak about his Saviour. Egbo Egbo was God's man, through and through.

Another fearless witness was Jimmy Mfon. Jimmy was about fifteen years old, athletic and intelligent. Like all the local lads he loved to swim, often in company with the white men at the close of day. But on that fateful occasion Samuel Bill was on the shore. He wrote afterwards:

'This has been a sad and sorrowful day, one of the saddest since coming here. Jimmy Mfon has lost his life while bathing in the river. A shark laid hold of him, tearing the flesh from his leg, right from the hip to the knee, laying the bone quite bare.

'The tragedy happened opposite the corner of our

house. I heard a fearful cry, and rushed down to the beach. He was unconscious; for besides the wound mentioned he had eight others. The mother was frantic with grief, and it seemed as if David Ekong could not stop crying. We all loved Jimmy. He was a bright and earnest follower of the Saviour. Next Sabbath he would have sat down with us at the Lord's table. Now he beholds his Redeemer's face.'

The funeral took place the following day, and that evening Sam entered in his diary: 'Buried Jimmy this morning. There was a large gathering, all deeply attentive, as I spoke of the resurrection and Second Coming of our Lord. I took the last look at dear Jimmy's face that I shall get, until I meet him on that great Day.'

Jimmy's death brought unexpected strengthening to the infant church. The little circle of Christians began to pray earnestly for his mother and brother, and soon both became believers. His chum, Equolo, had often listened to the Gospel but hesitated to commit himself, until the river tragedy set him thinking – 'Jimmy has gone to be with Jesus, whom he loved. I want to go there too.'

In spite of his father's opposition, and being turned out of his home, Equolo persevered in the Christian way and became one of the Qua Iboe Church's first teachers and pastors.

During this period the physical and spiritual stamina of the young pioneers was being tested to the limit. As Archie Bailie later recalled: 'I think of those three years Sam and I had together before he left for furlough. Often, when our bodies were racked with continuous attacks of fever, and we were unable to rise through sheer weakness, the Ibunos crowded to our house. Some would pray; more persuade us to eat, while others would gladly bring the oft-called-for water. When differences in our languages prevented conversation, it did not prevent big tears of sympathy from rolling down those dusky cheeks.'

Shared sorrows and dangers were forging strong links between God's servants and the people to whom He had sent them. They were also deepening their appreciation of each other, and of their high calling, as a typical quotation from Sam Bill's diary reveals: 'Archie and I have had a pleasant walk and talk; indeed we have had many of them, talking of old times and friends. We were taking a look into the future this evening. The outlook is dark if we leave faith out of the reckoning – but we cannot do that. God help us to keep above the sordid thoughts of the worldling, and understand something of the grandeur and nobility of our calling.'

CHAPTER FIVE

God's Seal

'God who has commissioned us . . . has put His seal upon us.' 2 Cor. 1:21-22.

The morning of December 29 1889 dawned dark and gloomy. Over the palm forest lay a thick pall of sand, carried south from the Sahara by an unusually strong harmattan wind.

Down by the riverside a crowd of Ibunos had gathered for the second baptismal service to take place in Qua Iboe. Old and young, slaves and freemen, chiefs and commoners, watched quietly as five of their number publicly confessed Christ as Saviour and Lord.

'Happy day, happy day, when Jesus washed my sins away,' sang the new believers – onlookers joining in as best they could. Then they made their way to the little church to praise God from full hearts. By the time their service was over the sun had broken through and the sky was blue and cloudless.

'How significant!' commented Archie Bailie. 'Surely the withering harmattan of an idolatrous worship thickly covered this people. But the rays of the Sun of Righteousness are beginning to penetrate and be felt.'

Six weeks later Sam Bill described the first observance of the Lord's Supper: 'Eleven of us sat down to the Table – all looking to Jesus as our common Saviour. Mr. Bailie spoke from Isaiah 53. Afterwards we partook of the emblems of our Lord's broken body and shed blood. There were about a hundred people in the church, and they were most orderly and attentive. It was a blessed time.'

Among the new communicants that February day were Chief Egbo Egbo, John Nwaining, and two elderly wives of a heathen chief. One sweltering afternoon the women had arrived at the mission house.

'We decided to leave the ju-ju, and follow Jesus, on the day of Etia's and David's baptism,' they told the wondering missionaries. 'How could we stand before the Son of God, and tell Him that we heard about His death for our sins, but that we would not believe?'

That evening Sam Bill recorded his feelings: 'What glorious news was this, this afternoon – our blessed Lord answering our prayers, and setting His seal on our work. I rejoice when any of these people show a desire to follow Jesus. But when I find these poor, down-trodden women, into whose lives scarcely a ray of joy ever enters, when I see them bringing their burdens to Calvary, when I see the rays of the Redeemer's glory piercing the thick darkness of their souls, then my heart is touched to its innermost depths.

'Often as I preach the blessed news of pardon for guilty sinners, looking the while into the earnest up-turned faces of these burdened women, I feel as if I would like to draw them all by sheer force, to the feet of Jesus, to get the peace they need.'

The responsiveness of the womenfolk made Sam long all the more, for the day when Grace would join him at Ibuno. It was not considered wise for a white man to stay longer than two years for his first tour in that fever-ridden climate, and he was giving much thought to ways and means of getting home.

'I am thinking how soon I may be joined to her I love,' he confided to his diary. 'Archie has given me £3 towards my fare, but my castle-building now and again gets a rude shock by the terrible thought that sufficient money may not come, and I shall have to stay here.'

The money did come, however, and not only enough for his own passage but a gift of £10 to enable David Ekong to accompany him. By now David's father had died, and it was evident that the Holy Spirit was at work in the young man, enlightening and equipping him to be God's messenger to his own people. Other Nigerian Christians had accompanied Scottish missionaries on furlough, and Sam looked forward with intense pleasure to introducing David to his friends at home.

On June 6 1890, after a final time of prayer with Archie, the travellers set out to join the steamer at Calabar. They arrived in Liverpool on a Sunday – 'having no clothes fit to appear in in public, much less in church.' It was an ordeal to face the bustle of city life, but faith was flowing strong and Sam's secret prayer that day reveals the hope in his heart: 'May my Heavenly Father bless my stay at home to the establishment of the Qua Iboe Mission.'

From Liverpool they proceeded to London – and Gracie. There were questions in Sam's mind. It seemed so long since they had met, and then so briefly. Letters had been exchanged as frequently as the mail-boat permitted, but how would it be when they met again? He need not have worried. They were meant for each other. With the approval of Mrs. Guinness and Grace's guardian, the wedding was fixed for October 14 in Mountpottinger Presbyterian Church, Belfast.

In the meantime Sam and David were meeting interested friends in London and Belfast. The boy was warmly received, his courteous bearing and obvious love for his Lord provoking the general reaction – 'If this is a typical Qua Iboe Christian, then we must see to it that this Mission is not hampered by lack of support.'

For David it was a wonderful experience to worship in beautiful churches and meet so many people who had prayed for him – but, oh, the agony of feet accustomed to freedom and now constricted in a pair of stout boots! There was little money for tram fares, and as they trudged mile after mile along hard city pavements Sam could see that the lad was near to tears. Those were the times when both longed for the creeks and sandy paths of Ibuno, but the contacts then made were used by God to answer their prayers for the establishment of His supply base.

When Sam Bill first set out for Africa he had hopes of supporting himself by trading and growing his own food. Neither of these ideas proved feasible. It would have been impossible to compete with the traders already operating, and anyway there were far more important things to be done. As to farming, the soil was so poor that even local people had to buy yams, cassava and other basic produce from more fertile areas. No cattle could survive the disease-bearing tsetse flies – so there was no milk, butter or beef.

Fish was sometimes obtainable, and the missionaries' shotgun supplied many a bird or small animal for the stock-pot But to supplement their own diet and help feed their house-boys, quantities of rice, flour and tinned stuffs had to be purchased, as well as building materials and clothing. Some of these came from the United Africa Company's factory at Eket, whose English agent, Mr. Harford, was always helpful. Other items could be bought in Calabar, but still more had to be shipped from Britain. All this was expensive, but Sam had no fears about daily provision.

'God has promised to supply all our need,' he wrote. 'Is this a needful thing, and will it further His work, and be for His glory? If we are convinced that these things are so, then let us regard this promise as a cheque on the Bank of England.'

God's supplies came in surprising ways. Once, the purchase of rice and trade biscuits for the boys resulted in a bill for £4 from the factory at Eket. Scraping up every available coin, the young pioneer still found himself short, so at prayers that evening the need was brought to the Heavenly Father. Next day the balance came – given voluntarily by the boys from their own meagre earnings.

For a year after arrival, Sam's only form of transport was a borrowed canoe. Just before Archie joined him he was offered a ship's dinghy for £4. It was exactly what he needed, but he could only raise a quarter of the modest price. The new missionary proved to be more affluent. He had £3, so together, they bought the little boat which was to carry them and their loads for many years up and down the river.

In the homeland, too, God was laying His channels. Harley College could give no help after the first year, but in Belfast a few loyal friends had banded themselves together as the Qua Iboe Missionary Association. They were humble folk, connected with the Island Street Mission Hall, which Sam and Archie had helped to build and where they had served as secretary and treasurer. The departure of the two young men to London, and then to Africa, had aroused keen interest and fervent prayer. Sacrificial giving was the natural outcome of such deep involvement.

The Association's first gift had reached Qua Iboe at an opportune time and Sam wrote gratefully: 'We have never been so hard up for food since coming to the mission field, as during the last month. Our tea, milk, sugar, flour, and all our tinned meats are finished. Sometimes for days we cannot get any fish, while yams, our staple vegetable, are not to be had, except at such a high price as precludes our purchasing them. So you see we sometimes fast! ... It is true, as you say, that £70 is small, placed against the great need, but it far exceeds our expectation of what would be done in the first year of the Society's existence. With such men engaged, heart and hand, to help us, and with the Risen One Himself pledged to abide with us always, what have we to fear? Truly nothing but the unbelief of our own hearts, and the false fears and doubts that arise therefrom. May God indeed deliver us from them all.'

For the second box-opening in January 1891, Samuel Bill and David Ekong were present in person in the Island Street Hall. Nothing could have been more stimulating to the faith and determination of their faithful supporters. It was clear that God's favour was upon the Qua Iboe Mission, and that it would continue to grow, so a proposal was made that a Council be formed, incorporating representatives of the Association, together with new friends who were coming forward to share responsibility.

Samuel Bill's prayer was being answered, but he recognised, and would acknowledge throughout his life, that the Mission was a channel and not a source, 'Bless God for the new society and for all the channels of supply,' he wrote. 'But, amid all, may God save us from trusting in any arm of flesh, even though it be one raised up by Himself. Our strength is in a prayer-hearing God and His promises are real. Without them the present and the future would be very cheerless.'

During the past months Samuel Bill had been living under considerable pressure and, since their October wedding, he and Grace had been constantly busy with visits and meetings in London and Ireland. Their friends saw that they needed a break, which they could not afford. Sam recorded with gratitude: 'The first act of the new Council was to send us away to Portrush, for

47

rest and holiday. They sent us to a fine hotel there, paying all expenses.'

After more meetings in Scotland, Dublin and Belfast it was time to prepare for leave-taking. Sam was much encouraged. Someone had given him an artesian pump, another a second-hand organ. Some interested doctors had supplied surgical instruments and medical books. A group had purchased a bell to summon the Ibunos to worship, and the steamship company had offered three return passages for the price of one.

The three travellers took part in an enthusiastic fare-well meeting, and a crowd of well-wishers gathered at the dock to give them a good send-off. Sam's diary entry that night reflected his mixed emotions: 'Bade goodbye to many, including Archie Bailie's old father. Tears stood in his eyes as I left him and it was difficult to restrain my own. Had a splendid prayer meeting down the quay, in one of the empty offices. The power of God was there. We felt He was sending us and that we had the full sympathy and prayers of His people. It was hard to say goodbye to Mother, and my dear ones. My poor mother was almost broken-hearted. She gives up so much for Jesus and gives it willingly. . . . He Who was born of a woman will understand.'

Despite the heartaches, Sam Bill was returning with confidence to his appointed task. God's seal of approval was on the Mission at home as well as on the field, and He was sending His servant back with two fellow-workers of the highest calibre – Gracie Bill and David Ekong.

CHAPTER SIX

The Eye of Faith

'By faith ... he looked forward to the city which has foundations, whose builder is God.' Heb 11:9–10.

On January 10 1892, a party was in full swing at Ibuno Mission House in honour of Samuel Bill's twenty-ninth birthday. Opposite him at the table sat Gracie, and between them four of their best friends – Chief Egbo Egbo and his wife, David Ekong, and John Nwaining. They were a happy group, united in love for Jesus Christ, and for one another in His service, and they were full of praise for answered prayer.

It was just over six months since Sam had introduced his bride to Ibuno. Grace had heard so much about the place that it was like coming home. But she was a gently-reared girl, and the primitive conditions of life cannot have been easy to accept at that time. Passing through Calabar they had arranged for a Scottish nurse to come early in December for the expected confinement. In October a letter was received saying she was unable to fulfil her promise – shattering news, for by this time Gracie was far from well. An SOS to a Calabar doctor brought word that he could not come without permission, which would take a fortnight to obtain.

The mother-to-be was now alarmingly ill with asthma, and three days later gave birth to a five-weeks'-premature baby girl. It was a nightmare for the young father, forced to act as doctor and midwife, without

49

even the support of Archie Bailie, who by now had gone on furlough to claim his own bride.

'It was a terrible week,' Sam admitted, 'and the situation entirely new to me. Everything was dark except to the eye of faith.'

On November 4 a substitute nurse arrived – 'never was anyone more welcome'. A week later Grace was still so weak and breathless that for three nights in succession, she had to sit propped up in a deck chair by the bedside. The nurse sent for another doctor, but by the time he came the patient had begun to improve.

'There's really nothing I can do,' he said. 'It will take time and good nourishing food to get her strong again.'

Before she had fully recovered, her exhausted husband succumbed to the dreaded blackwater fever. His diary for December 23 1891 records: 'A month has passed since I made an entry in this book. Since then I have had one of the most dangerous diseases, haematuric fever. Through the blessing of God, and the careful and unceasing nursing of dear Gracie, I am still alive. 'When I was at my worst, the Christians held a prayer meeting three times a day. David was away when I took ill, but he got news of it and started immediately for home. To reach here he had to paddle the canoe for I don't know how many hours, and then walk thirty miles along the sand. He reached us, footsore and weary, in the middle of the night. I often thank God for David.'

By Christmas the worst of the ordeal was over. Baby Emma was thriving and, as Sam recalled: 'In spite of all our troubles we had a happy Christmas. Mrs. Bill was getting stronger and made a big plum pudding. Mr. Harford sent down a big joint of beef and we had a good dinner. We illuminated the yard and, in spite of the chop flies, the boys and girls had a great time at Blind Man's Buff. Four days later Mr. Harford came down with the launch and an invitation to spend a few days

"I often thank God for David."

at Eket. We gladly went, though Grace had to stay up half the night packing. No doubt a baby does take a dreadful lot of work!'

The unexpected change and rest was a loving Father's provision for His children, and they returned refreshed, ready to re-open the school and dispensary, and to prepare another batch of candidates for baptism. So, as Sam Bill entered on his thirtieth year, there were many reasons for thanksgiving – and the Plan was still unfolding.

As Sam had foreseen, Grace loved the Ibuno women and children, and was loved by them in return. In spite of the baby and she herself being laid low by intermittent fever, she taught in the school and was in constant demand at the little dispensary. She was appalled by the physical needs of the people. Malaria was endemic. Pneumonia and rheumatism flourished in the damp atmosphere, and a huge proportion of the population suffered from tropical yaws and ulcers.

Accidents were common. Men fell from palm trees on the sharp machetes they carried to cut down the fruit for oil-making. Large cooking pots overbalanced, scalding the small children playing nearby. People rolled over in their sleep and were burned by the red-hot embers of the evening fires. Worst of all were the sufferings of the women at the hands of midwives with no knowledge of the basic laws of hygiene. Having had some training in midwifery, 'Mma Bill', as they called Grace, was often summoned to assist at abnormal deliveries.

Usually the patients could return home, coming back for daily dressings or treatment, but some, with pneumonia or other serious conditions, needed constant attention, and Gracie's strength was often stretched to the limit, as she wrestled with poultices in the heat of the day. Two years after her arrival in Qua Iboe, Mrs. Bill, with her small daughter and infant son, was carried aboard the home-bound steamer. Her husband accompanied her as far as Accra, reluctantly leaving her there to continue the journey with an Ibuno girl, Mary Egbo Egbo, to look after the children.

It was a hard parting but not a fruitless one, for when Gracie regained her strength, she toured Ireland north and south, addressing many gatherings with unusual eloquence and spiritual power. 'Towns on every hand are pleading for teachers,' she would say. 'Back myself from the valley of the shadow of death, compelled to leave the work I would gladly die for, with all my heart and soul I appeal to some of the young men of our land to step into the breach which sickness has made in our ranks. Jesus Himself said, "I must work ... the night cometh when no man can work." '

One youth who could not dismiss from his mind the fragile mother and her burning words was John Kirk. By the time Grace Bill returned to Africa, he was ready to accompany her. He fitted eventually into the third mission station, according to Gracie's husband, 'like a round peg in a round hole.'

Meanwhile at Ibuno, Sam had been extremely busy. During furlough he had shared his vision for an Industrial Branch where young men could be trained to earn a living and, at the same time, meet the building requirements of a growing church and mission. There was no local stone or clay suitable for brick-making, so he had conceived the idea of a saw-mill, to make use of the abundant supply of timber. The project was sympathetically considered by the Home Council, who reckoned that a steam-operated mill could be bought and shipped for £150. Only £35 was readily available and they decided that if another £20 came in before Mrs. Bill left Ireland, this could be taken as a sign of divine approval. The unexpected reduction of passage money and a farewell offering of £22 removed all doubt, and the order had been duly placed.

Some months later the saw-mill reached its destination, to be unpacked and erected before the incredulous eyes of the Ibunos. Seven boys were taken on to serve a four-year apprenticeship, among them Thomas Akpan, a promising young man who had been led to Christ by his cousin, David Ekong.

The first church building was beginning to crumble under the attacks of ants, and the Christians had been wishing they could replace it with a more permanent structure. Money was the problem for they were very poor, and materials were costly. The saw-mill altered the whole situation. Taking their example from Etubom, they set to work felling trees, hauling them through the bush and towing them down-river to Ibuno. Even the women took part, going to the mangrove swamps to procure huge headloads of firewood for the boilers. A large number of planks were soon prepared, and over £50 contributed towards the purchase of corrugated iron, bolts and nails.

The site was the next question to be decided. About a mile up-river from the mission house, in the most central town of the Ibuno area, was the principal idol temple of which David Ekong's grandfather had been high priest. The old man had died, and the new owners decided to give it for the building of a church. So on this ground, thick with the bones and relics of ancient sacrifice, a church capable of seating 500 people was erected to the glory of God.

At the same time its first pastor was being prepared for office. It was when Samuel Bill was gravely ill, that David Ekong began to preach in public. Now he and other young men were conducting meetings in the yards of the chiefs where great crowds gathered to listen. Several notable conversions had taken place, and members were being added daily to Mr. Bill's class for inquirers. He was just recovering from a bad bout of fever when he wrote: 'Was able to take my class this afternoon – and what a class! Truly the Spirit of God is working in Ibuno in a way, and on a scale, never experienced before. The people crowded into the hall today until we had to take some of the furniture out; then the back verandah was filled and a number on the front one.... The sight of so many, old and young, with such earnest faces, stirred me so deeply that I could scarcely command my voice to pray or speak to them. Praise God for these tokens of His presence. May this day of salvation not pass until many Ibunos have been brought savingly to Jesus.'

A number of chiefs and other influential men, who

attended inquirers' class, had given up trading in rum and gin, with the result that the empty bottles, once used for medicine, were now in short supply! While rejoicing in the transformation, Samuel Bill was aware of the perils of rapid growth, and his own need of discernment. He wrote: 'It is very possible to have a heart knowledge of Christ, and yet be able, in very small measure, to define the doctrines which are the embodiment of the great plan of salvation. He who would show sinners the way must have a clear view and firm grip of them, but what I need, and what these people need most of all, is to see and know Christ. If their eyes are fixed on Him, their lives will be transformed. There is a danger of them coming to look on communicants' classes, baptisms, prayer meetings and the building of churches as the kernel of their religion, while it is, indeed, only the husk. We need more spiritual light by which alone true spiritual life can be discerned.'

The last night of 1896 found Mr. Bill looking back with praise, and forward with hope: 'Another year gone – almost. It has been very full of work, and the blessing of the Lord has been everywhere . . . O Lord! Do Thou take charge of us through the coming year, and teach us more of Thyself and of Thy will. Make us more like Thee, and let us see the mighty working of Thy grace amongst us.'

CHAPTER SEVEN

The Epic of 'Evangel'

'No good thing does the Lord withold from those who walk uprightly.' Ps. 84:11.

Nature and grace combined to make Friday, November 25 1898 a red-letter day. The rainy season was over for another year, but the cloudless blue sky had not yet become brazen with heat, and a riot of tropical blossom was mirrored in the Qua Iboe river as the brand-new launch, 'Evangel', steamed north on her maiden voyage. On board were six thankful people – two Bills, two Bailies, John Kirk and Edward Heaney, the latest recruit to the missionary team.

Skipper Bill was in his element. Transport had been a major problem during the past eleven years. With no roads, and a maze of creeks and swamps, the only way to get around was by canoe, and, as the mission developed, heavier and heavier loads of building materials, food and medical supplies had to be carried from Eket to the various centres. The agent had been generous in lending the company launch and granting free passages for missionaries, but the situation was far from satisfactory; and he might not always be there.

It was over four years since the matter had first been discussed with Home Council. The purchase of a launch was a big item, but their decision to go ahead in faith was confirmed by an offer from interested workmen in a Belfast shipyard to do the building in their spare time.

An enthusiastic start had been made, when a fire in the yard brought delays which lasted until dark winter evenings made work impossible. Months passed into years and almost every mail brought news of some fresh problem. Meantime, Samuel Bill's health was suffering through frequent drenchings, and he came to dread the twenty-mile canoe journeys to Okat, where the Bailies had established a second mission station.

In June 1897, Sam went on another up-river reconnaisance, accompanied by John Kirk. This time they went as far as the first bridge, judging the distance to be about sixty miles.

'The population becomes much denser and the land higher and richer,' he noted. 'We visited a good many towns, some not visited before by white men, and in all told the "Old Story". In every place we received quiet and reverent attention, and in some a pressing invitation to return soon.'

'One thing which impressed me deeply was the extensive field there is for wise and careful effort among these people. The door is open, and they are ready for the preaching of glad tidings. Our great need is for the launch, that we may be able to carry out this work, but I have promised that I will go back, whether the launch comes or not, and keep in touch with them.

'Another thing that struck me was the large number of Ibunos that spend most of their time at the markets. We had many happy little services among them. I hope, when the launch comes, to spend as much time as I can get away from this place itinerating up-river.'

Over a year later a letter arrived stating that the craft was now ready.

'I could have shouted "Hallelujah!" ' said the usually undemonstrative Sam.

The thirty-four foot launch had received a big send-off from Belfast Lough. Some hundreds of well-wishers gathered on the beach at Helen's Bay and, after a dedicatory prayer by the Moderator of the Presbyterian Church in Ireland, Samuel Bill's mother was called upon to name the vessel. Her announcement of the 'Evangel' was greeted by hearty cheering and the raising of a flag bearing the name in bold letters. The brief ceremony was brought to a close with the singing of the hymn 'All hail the power of Jesus' Name' – and the little launch steamed off, soon afterwards to be shipped from Liverpool.

News of her departure brought mounting excitement and a measure of trepidation to Samuel Bill. 'I note that the launch is to be under my control and supervision,' he wrote. 'Well, I accept that responsibility with pleasure, but also with fear and trembling. So many untoward circumstances have occurred in her history already! Yet, I believe the Lord will have her in His keeping. I think she must be precious in His eyes. When I think of all the faith and prayers, the troubles and waitings, the generous gifts, and self-sacrifices of His children to provide her and send her out, I feel He will take care of her and make her a blessing. I will do my part to the best of my ability in caring for her that she may do her work.'

The prospective skipper was at Okat when the message came that the vessel had arrived, and he set off at once with Archie Bailie, and four boys, on what proved to be an eventful expedition.

'We reached Opobo, after paddling all night through the creeks. The steamer lay at anchor and beside her we saw a steam launch – the long-looked-for 'Evangel'! What a pleasant sight it was for our eyes and how eager we were to explore her!'

All was not to be plain sailing, however. The first trouble was a faulty pump.

Commented Mr. Bill, 'There is no use numbering them, for there was nothing but trouble till we reached Qua Iboe.'

Tired out with improvising and adapting, they lay down to sleep, anticipating an early start in the morning. By daylight, steam was up, ready to catch the high tide to clear the shallow 'Flats'. They had not travelled twenty yards before sticking, so decided to try another route, only to go aground on a sandbank about a hundred yards from the breakers.

They might as well have tried to move a mountain as to re-float 'Evangel'. The strong current kept pressing the launch against the bank, while the sand silted up around her, and the pump refused to work. To add to the problems they had no fresh water, having reckoned on getting plenty in the creek, and most of their provisions had been sent ahead in the canoe with two of the boys. However, they were able to collect firewood, and great quantities of crabs which they boiled in salt water. By the time their meal was over, the tide was on the turn.

'As the waters rose our fears also rose, knowing that, when it was high enough the breakers would roll right up to where we were lying. As the water got rougher the launch began to bump, and every bump went to our hearts.'

There was no alternative but to go full steam ahead with the tide, and pray for a miracle to set them free. The miracle happened. 'Words fail me to describe the feeling of relief when once we felt her going forward,' said Sam.

Soon they found the canoe, half-submerged among the coiling roots of the strange, salt-loving mangrove trees, while its occupants struggled to rescue the contents from complete destruction. Men and boys had had as much as they could take for one day, and sought refuge with a friendly chief, who provided anchorage, food and shelter for the night.

'We slept the sleep of utter exhaustion,' continued Samuel Bill. 'In the morning we set our minds again to the problem of getting home. It was now clear that the launch, which was to draw 3ft 3ins, draws 4ft 6ins. Had we known this we would not have tried the creeks at all. So we now resolved to try crossing the Opobo and Qua Iboe river Bars.'

All day was spent in preparation for the big attempt. The white men at Opobo counselled against the venture, as did the chief, but Sam Bill was not easily daunted. God had provided this vessel. It was desperately needed to maintain His work. There was no other route open so, he reasoned, it must be right to go ahead. Committing themselves to God's keeping, they set out early next morning, crossing the Opobo Bar, and steaming along the coastline till darkness fell about them.

'There was nothing for it but to put down anchor. Mr Bailie and I had been miserably sick all day. We got some food cooked, but could not look at it. From the look of the sky a tornado was coming, so we lay down on the little grating aft, with no very comfortable feelings. The sea got rough with the evening breeze and the water began to splash over us. We got up and put on raincoats and rainboots and lay down again, so sick we did not care much what happened to us.

'At 2.30 a.m. we roused the boys – who were in no higher spirits than ourselves – to get a fire on, and steam up, against daylight. By 5.30 a.m. we were under way, and it was not long before we came in sight of the Bar and the breakers. Our steam was now up to 80 lbs. On we came, seasickness forgotten, as we drew near. Soon we saw the channel. It was smooth. Tremendous rollers were riding past us, but not breaking. That was the all-important part.

'As we approached, I took hold of the line, and commenced throwing it. Three fathoms . . . three fathoms . . . still three fathoms . . . another throw – two fathoms and a half . . . then two fathoms . . . twice more, two fathoms . . . the next throw – two and a half fathoms . . . then three fathoms – and we knew we were over! A cheer broke from all on board. What relief and satisfaction were in that cheer! We were as good as home, and in another half hour were at the mission beach.

'We had a warm welcome. The canoe had got home by the creeks, bringing news that we intended trying the Bar, so they had been on the look-out for us. That evening at our prayer meeting the Christians all joined with us in thanking God for our deliverance and safe arrival. Since then we have had a special prayer meeting, thanking our Heavenly Father for providing our little vessel and commending it to His care for the future. May it indeed be precious in His sight and used greatly in the spread of His Kingdom up-river.'

The 'Evangel' had arrived in the nick of time to transport John Kirk and his belongings to a new mission centre at Etinan. Since that first visit, almost eighteen months ago, there had been repeated requests for a resident teacher, and the people had gone to amazing lengths to prove the sincerity of their invitation. On November 11, viewing the little house they had prepared so carefully, Sam had found it impossible to put them off again. John Kirk was coming back from leave. There was no word of the launch but, somehow or other, they would have to get a big enough canoe to bring him and his belongings up for at least a couple of weeks.

'I don't know how I'll do it,' he had admitted, 'But God will open up the way for me to bring you a teacher this day fortnight.'

And here they were, to the very day, steaming up to Etinan in 'Evangel'.

Mr. Bill described their reception: 'At Mr. K's future residence, fresh and pleasant surprises were in store for us. A neat yard had been enclosed with a strong wooden fence at the back of the house. In one corner of this a place had been cleared for a bathroom, and all the back verandah had been floored with beaten clay. At either end a couch had been formed of the same material, and in front of the couches, a table – all beaten very hard, and so strong and straight that it had all the appearance of cement work.

'Mrs. Bailie and Mrs. Bill were with us on this expedition and they created real surprise and wonder in the town, the people following and whispering loudly 'Women! Women!' We said goodbye to Mr. Kirk and came away, leaving the people delighted that they had at last obtained their hearts' desire – a teacher.'

CHAPTER EIGHT

The First Pillars

'They . . . who were reputed to be pillars, gave . . . the right hand of fellowship.' Gal. 2:9.

'Having considered the duties and responsibilities of the office of elder, are you willing to undertake them heartily?'

'I am,' came the quiet but firm response.

'Do you engage to take the Word of God as your rule in all matters, even though it may entail pecuniary or other loss on yourself, and the forsaking of old customs?'

'I do.'

'Do you accept this work as a call from God – so that, while human instrumentality has been used in choosing and appointing you, you reckon yourselves as called indeed by the Holy Ghost to oversee the Church of God, in accordance with Acts 20:28?'

'I do.'

Samuel Bill studied the serious faces of the eight men standing reverently before him in Ibuno church. Around them were gathered over three hundred baptised believers, almost half of whom had been admitted to church membership during the past year. The big increase in inquirers and candidates for baptism had underlined the need for elders, and he was well satisfied with the 'eight of our best members of longest standing and most blameless life' who had been chosen, and were now being set apart to this high office.

Until this time, when problems arose, he had called all the members together, read the relevant Scriptures, and discussed with them what action should be taken. It was a cumbersome procedure and he felt that these elders should be able to decide most matters, reserving the church gatherings for specially important issues. Each of them had shown concern for the needy and zeal in witnessing, so their ordination was merely a recognition of gifts already given by God.

Three of the new elders were engaged in full-time Christian work and being supported by the church. David Ekong, now married to Mary Egbo Egbo, was virtually pastor of the Ibuno church, where he preached every Sunday with power and winsomeness. John Nwaining, married to David's sister, was pastoring the growing church at Big Town.

Then there was Abasi Mfon, the dispensary assistant who accompanied Mr. Bill to Ireland in 1896. Recently a request had come for him to go as teacher/preacher across the river to the town of Okorotip, of which Archie Bailie had once written – 'Oh what darkness covers that place! They would not listen to the Gospel, and told us plainly they did not want to hear. They said it was cloth they wanted, and rum and food, and if we did not bring these things they did not want us back.' In spite of this unfavourable reception the Christians had continued to visit, and now Abasi had moved, with his wife and family, to live and serve in Okorotip in the name of Christ.

Another elder-elect was Thomas Akpan. By this time he was foreman of the Industrial Branch and largely through his influence, three more apprentices had become followers of the carpenter of Nazareth. He also taught in day and evening school, preaching regularly in three villages and accepting, for the sake of the Gospel, considerably lower pay than he could have earned in Government employment. Beside him stood the stately Chief Egbo Egbo and his kinsman Ibok, men whose lives and homes bore eloquent testimony to the transforming power of God.

As they answered the questions, and took their vows, Sam gave humble and fervent thanks for the calibre of these first office bearers who would set a standard for coming years, not only at Ibuno, but throughout the extending Qua Iboe Church.

In releasing Abasi Mfon to go to Okorotip, Samuel Bill had left himself without a reliable helper who, with increasing experience, could have relieved him and Grace of much routine dispensing. Beginning again with a raw recruit would make it very difficult to get away for the up-river itineration which he envisaged with the coming of 'Evangel'. But, if he was tied, the Word was not bound, and, in strange ways, needy people were brought to his very doorstep.

Ibuno mission house had become known far and wide as 'Ufok Erinyanga' – the 'House of Help'. The church people too were earning a reputation for hospitality. Sometimes their guests were new believers from other districts, coming to taste Christian fellowship for the first time. Sometimes they were refugees, arriving un-expectedly and begging shelter on their homeward way.

Early in 1899 a large party appeared, emaciated and bedraggled, on the beach in front of the mission house. Mr. Bill counted them – twenty-one men and over a hundred women and children. They were a pitiful sight, and their story was a sad one.

Three hundred miles north, in their home territory, they had been tricked by one of their own witch-doctors, and sold to Arab slavers. In the usual brutal manner they were yoked together with forked sticks, and marched long distances into the interior. Those whose strength proved unequal to the journey were left to die by the roadside, or their sufferings summarily ended by the thrust of a spear, or blow of a club.

From one town to another the survivors were sold, until they found themselves eventually near Calabar. Weak as they were, the desire for freedom was still strong. By means of their owners' canoes they escaped down the Cross river, leaving them there to walk on the sand along the coast, till they reached Qua Iboe country.

Sam described their reception: 'House space was sorely taxed during the six weeks of their sojourn with us. Our new sawhouse and workshop held a good many, and a kitchen and two outhouses a few more, while the neighbours all about were very kind, putting up as many as they could. We were able to give them some work – shifting sand and levelling a place to make a little railway, and filling up a large hole in front of the Mission House. The men cut firewood for the launch, and gathered palm nuts from which they made oil. Some made paddles and sold them to the Ibunos, and in one way and another they managed to get food from day to day.'

A Government expedition was then in the area, opening up roads and enforcing laws to ban inter-tribal warfare and human sacrifice. At the request of the refugees, their unhappy plight was explained to the British Consul through the major in charge of the soldiers. Soon afterwards two large canoes arrived, with an order to get the runaway slaves on board as quickly as possible.

'So they are gone,' Sam reported, 'and will no doubt reach the place from which cruelty and greed drove them a few years ago. We are glad to have them away, as food was becoming a problem. A sad point was the very few children among them. Death had claimed most of the little ones. The hardships of the way were too great for them, so most of the parents were childless.'

No one stayed at Ibuno without hearing the Gospel, and many a refugee had cause to thank God for the tribulation which brought him to a new freedom in Christ.

At the turn of the century the whole country seemed to be opening up to the Gospel. There was obvious need for more missionaries, but Samuel Bill was reluctant to make widespread appeals, dreading the recruitment of mis-fits. 'I leave the matter in God's hand,' he wrote. 'He knows exactly what is needed, and I am confident that, if He sees another man should come out here, He will send one. If a suitable man applies, then I think Council should accept him as from God.'

He went on to describe the sort of worker needed to relieve him at Ibuno for his forthcoming furlough. In addition to being spiritually mature, he would require 'To be able to set forth the Gospel clearly and simply. He should be able to take charge of the school occasionally, and have a taste for medical work. He should be able to take charge of the apprentices; not necessarily be a tradesman but able to take an intelligent interest in their work. He would also need to be a man who would count it no hardship to be up every morning and ready for work, at 6 a.m.'

It seemed a tall order but, in far-off Londonderry the Lord of the harvest was preparing His man for the job. Mr. Bill had already met him and formed a high opinion of the young teacher who was acting as the Mission's local secretary. News of his application to join the missionary band was hailed with joy and, following a brief course in tropical medicine, R. L. McKeown arrived in Qua Iboe in November 1899.

'We brought him down to Ibuno that he might see the place, and that we might get all the home news,' wrote Samuel Bill. 'I cannot tell you how delighted we were to receive him – a real North of Ireland man. I do hope he will stand the climate. I am sure we shall all like him. He preached here and at Big Town and I enjoyed hearing him, for he puts the Gospel plainly and simply, just in the way that should reach the people.'

Robert McKeown, in turn, was writing home about his introduction to Ibuno: 'I could scarcely believe my senses as I saw how much has been done here, and if Mr. Bill were not the humblest of men he would be proud indeed.'

At this time Gracie was again facing the possibility of having to leave the work and the people she loved so dearly. Writing home she confessed: 'The flesh so shrinks from suffering and weakness, but in the midst of it all one realises God's hand, and that He makes no mistakes. The lesson for me this time seemed to be the surrender of even being here with Mr. Bill, and having to go home and *stay there*, but when (as far as I know it) with all my heart I said "Even that Lord, if it bring most glory to Thee", my health was given back to me. I believe that had Council not called us home, I would have been given strength to stay on till next year.'

Council had been wisely guided, for even before the Bills got away for furlough, Gracie was struck down again with blackwater fever. Robert McKeown feared that she would never survive the journey home.

'All Mrs. Bill's strength was gone,' he wrote. 'In fact every organ in her body seemed about finished. We could do nothing, only cry to God all the time; the elders met in the church and had special prayer for her. She passed a variable day but slept through the night and woke this morning decidedly better. With the continued blessing of God she may be carried aboard the steamer tomorrow ... The whole thing has been in answer to prayer, for Mrs. Bill was far beyond human help. As Mr. Heaney said to me – "The redemption of Africa is a costly business. And the reason poor Africa is so far from being redeemed is that it has cost us all so little".'

Before long R. L. McKeown, and his bride of a few months, had themselves experienced that cost. Early in May 1901, after taking charge at Ibuno during the Bills' absence, they were forced by ill-health to quit Africa. For them it was a permanent home-going – but not to retirement from the Qua Iboe Mission, for Mr. McKeown's experience of the hazards and hopes of missionary life prepared him for unique service as its first full-time general secretary. God's servants were proving that no suffering is wasted in the outworking of His Plan. Strong, straight pillars were as essential at the home base as in Qua Iboe.

CHAPTER NINE

All In the Plan

'Plans for welfare and not for evil, to give you a future and a hope.' Jer. 29:11.

Samuel Bill was possessed of a naturally buoyant spirit, but his heart sank to his boots the day he saw the launch submerged under 16 feet of water at Etinan beach.

Standing beside him, Archie Bailie watched his friend anxiously. He had broken the news about the sinking in a letter to the Bills before they landed at Calabar in July 1901. It was distressing that this should happen while Sam was on furlough, in view of the unremitting labour he had put into 'Evangel', and how desperately she was needed. How would he react?

He commented: 'She's a sorry sight, but if Council can send us out some chains we'll have a go at getting her up again.'

Months must pass before the raising tackle could arrive. In the meantime there was plenty to be done erecting the new printing press. For fourteen years Efik school books had been purchased from Calabar, but the steady increase of pupils convinced Mr. Bill that it was time for the Mission to have its own press. He knew nothing about printing but remedied that by arranging to attend a printing works in Belfast, where he learned how to set type, print, and bind books.

A small hand press was purchased, and accompanied

the returning missionaries on the steamer. Now it had to be assembled. In transit some unidentified rodent had nibbled the rollers. The stock of type was very limited, and no ink had been supplied. Nothing daunted, Sam's improvising instincts got to work and before long the patched rollers were turning out scores of primers.

As well as her usual duties in school and dispensary, Grace was now chief type-setter and two little girls helped her to sew up the finished 'Ikpats'. By all means, the continuing stream of new believers must be encouraged to learn to read the Word of God.

The sinking of the launch had not been the only bad news awaiting the return of the Bills. Smallpox had swept the area claiming, among many victims, Chief Egbo Egbo. Since his conversion the good chief had been active in applying Christian standards to his own community, and largely through his efforts, a number of reforms had been introduced, including the abolition of human sacrifice, trial by ordeal, and the killing of twin children. For a time he lost favour with the heathen people but, through tact and reasonableness, confidence was regained. When a native court was established at Ibuno he was appointed a magistrate, and elected its first president, renowned for fair and wise judgement.

During his last illness Egbo Egbo's great concern was lest, in delirium, he might unconsciously call upon an evil spirit for help. In spite of severe suffering, however, he had died triumphantly, with the name of Jesus on his lips. Neither church nor town seemed the same to the Bills without the tall figure of their friend but in both circles his life had left an indelible mark for God.

Early in the new year preparations began for lifting the launch. The problem was considerable. Unladen, the craft was known to weigh seven tons; filled with water and sand it was at least double that weight. To augment the totally inadequate gear now on its way from Belfast, Sam decided to construct a large wooden tank, measuring 17 feet by 10 feet by 3 feet, which he calculated should have a lifting capacity of 20 tons.

As soon as winch and chains arrived, Sam, Archie, and Thomas Akpan set off for Etinan with as much manpower as they could muster. Their plan, to float the tank over 'Evangel', proved impossible because of her funnel. Strenuous efforts to remove this were frustrated by snags of river weed.

Defeated and baffled, with hands raw from hauling the ropes and chains, Samuel Bill returned to Ibuno. The pastor was ill so, although extremely tired and fighting off a chill, he had to prepare to preach on Sunday. It was hard to concentrate. 'Have had a miserable day thinking about the launch,' he recorded that night. 'I fear I might have done more to get it up – and the thought is intolerable.'

How could he go back to borrowing canoes and recruiting paddlers? How could he bear the sight of 'Evangel' under water every time he visited Etinan? Above all, how could he write home and tell the good people that their gift lay useless in the river bed? Surely if they could persevere they must succeed.

As he thought and prayed, strength flowed back into weary limbs, and by Sunday night his mind was made up to return shortly and give it another trial. 'Since arriving at this decision I feel much happier.'

Archie Bailie agreed to a further attempt, and Thomas again volunteered to do the diving. The scheme, this time was to build a square trap in the bottom of the tank to let the funnel come through. With great ingenuity this was accomplished, and Thomas dived under the stem and stern of the launch to secure chains which were then made fast to strong tree trunks, placed horizontally across the tank. After this the tank was filled with water, to lower it almost three feet into the river and nearer the deck of the sunken vessel. The chain slings were then tightened, and the large volume of water baled out of the tank, enabling its lifting power to operate.

Once the craft was moved off the river bed, Mr. Bill and his team of helpers winched and manoeuvred it into shallower water. Assisted by the daily tide, each lift raised it about three feet until, at the end of a week, 'Evangel' was hauled to the safety of a creek. There they commenced digging out the sand that filled the vessel to her skylights.

'This was the anxious and exciting time and we all worked like madmen,' wrote Samuel Bill. 'Would we get enough sand out to let her rise, before the tide covered our makeshift bacon-box combings? Great was our joy when we saw the bow rising slowly, then the deck, and gradually the stern. And none too soon, for the tide was making fast. The boiler seems none the worse, and the engine is not a bit rusted. Otherwise she is a wreck.'

Wreck or no wreck, 'Evangel' was afloat again. An immense job of re-building lay ahead, but as they took their homeward way, bruised, cut and dead beat, the men were satisfied. 'We could never have done it without Thomas,' was Mr. Bill's report to Home Council.

Gracie's health was again giving cause for concern. Soon after the launch episode she went to Calabar for examination, accompanied by a lady missionary. Her husband waited uneasily for the verdict.

'This has been a sad day' he wrote after her return. 'The doctor's report is that Grace must go home at once. The prospect is dark for the next three years. But it is all in the Plan and must be for the best. . . . We shall understand it some time.'

Within a fortnight she was on the steamer leaving

Sam to one of the loneliest periods he ever experienced – for Archie Bailie was also on furlough. Every little thing reminded him of Grace. Taking his nightly stroll on the verandah the sound of laughter from a neighbouring compound made him feel still more alone so he decided to shorten the long evening by going to bed early. Even then – 'I lay awake thinking of you till daylight.'

Nothing seemed to go right during those first few weeks of what Sam came to call 'the Year of the Exodus.' He had forgotten how to cook, and the boy's bread was inedible. Weevils infested the fusty flour; chop flies were biting fiercely and rats multiplied alarmingly in the ground-floor store. To make matters worse he developed toothache, and his varicose veins were unbearably painful.

As time went on, however, he was able to picture Grace with the children in Belfast and the situation began to make sense.

'Perhaps God saw that Emma needed you at home, and the aneurism is the way He took to force you back where you were most needed,' he wrote. 'It is quite possible that, when the need for you there passes, He will give us many years together yet in Qua Iboe. We can look forward to that, at any rate.'

Having got so far he took himself firmly in hand marched to the dispensary, mixed a stiff iron tonic, took the first dose, bandaged his swollen leg and began work.

The launch had to be rebuilt and the school, closed when Gracie left, had to be reopened. As usual, in both of these tasks Thomas was at his side.

A few months later Thomas lay dead. Looking at the peaceful face with its familiar little smile, Samuel Bill could hardly take it in. Thomas had been ill for a month, but only after three weeks was the seriousness of the condition apparent. Sam had decided to nurse him in the mission house, explaining to Grace: 'I think he will have a better chance with me – even humanly speaking – and I trust God may bless the remedies we use.'

The nursing was constant and heavy, but in spite of every attention and much earnest prayer, it was soon clear that Thomas would not recover. Conscious and serene to the end, he talked with his visitors, and assured them that he was not afraid, but glad to go. It was on Sunday that he died – 'A Sunday without a sermon, but not without a message.'

After the funeral, Samuel Bill sat down to write to the Mission secretary: 'I can hardly tell you how I feel. He has been my right-hand man in many things for many years and, apart from his wife and children, there is no one in Ibuno who will miss him as much as I. He was one of the first to follow the Lord and since that time, there was never a breath against his name.

'Thomas was my close friend, with whom I could talk over most matters. He was staunch and true, and could be trusted through thick and thin. His place will not be filled so far as I am concerned, nor so far as a certain branch of the work is concerned ... The Industrial Branch has had more to do with the success of the work than most would guess ... It is of concern, not only to Ibuno but to the whole Mission, to continue – but how without Thomas?'

Life had to go on. With little stomach for work Sam got back to the launch building. It would be good to have it in commission again, for this was the rainy season, and he was feeling again the effects of frequent soakings in the open canoe.

June brought good news. Archie Bailie would be out by the next boat! The needs of their small sons prevented his wife accompanying him and there had been some uncertainty about his return, but now he was coming. Sam was too excited to sleep that night after getting his mail. It would be a pleasant sight to see Archie again!

From 5 a.m. on July 28 he was on the lookout for the steamer, carrying the returning missionaries up to Eket. At eight o'clock the familiar hooter brought him dashing down to the beach for as close a view as possible. There they were, Archie and the two lady missionaries who had travelled with him, waving and calling from the deck. A few days later Sam made his way up to Okat, heard the home news, and beat Archie at a game of chess. It was like old times again.

Trouble was not all over, however. Within three weeks he received an urgent summons back to Okat. After walking for an hour and forty minutes, over a very bad road to get there in the shortest time, he arrived to find Archie rolling on the bed, gasping for breath, in the throes of a severe heart attack.

'Oh Sam, if only you felt it,' he groaned.

As each wave of pain broke over him it seemed as if he could not surface again. His friend, watching anxiously, knew there was little he could do to help. For a while the suffering abated, but as dawn was breaking another attack gripped him.

'I can't stand much more, Sam. Pray that God will take me soon.'

Sam was too numb to pray. He had been through a great deal in past months and the thought of losing Archie filled him with dismay. Believing the end to be imminent, he sent a messenger to Etinan to summon John Kirk and Edward Heaney. Before they could arrive he became aware of a crowd of people gathering quietly at the door. He recognised them as local Christians.

'Etubom,' said their leader, 'we would like to come in to pray for our teacher.'

There, around the sick man's bed, they poured out their confident petitions for his recovery. As Sam listened, his own faith strengthened, and he was able to join in claiming the healing power of God. Almost immediately the severe pain relaxed its grip. That night Archie Bailie slept, and although he had brief recurrences, the worst was over and he made a good recovery.

By Christmas time Mrs. Bailie had rejoined her husband and they were occupying the main bedroom at Ibuno mission house. In another room were the two ladies now in charge of the new Training Institute at Okat. A third room accommodated Kirk and Heaney who, in spite of opposition, were seeing a thriving church established at Etinan. Their host, displaced from his own bed to a stretcher in the hall, was delighted to have their company. The ladies took over the catering and tackled a backlog of mending from his neglected wardrobe.

'I'm ashamed to let them do so much, but very glad of their help,' he confided in his letter to Grace, adding wistfully, 'It all made me think long and wish you were here.'

It would be another year before Sam's furlough brought them together again. Later generations would condemn such prolonged separation as placing an unsupportable strain on any marriage, but Sam and Gracie Bill accepted it without question, as part of the cost of unreserved commitment. Wherever each might be they were still united, in the purpose and plan of God.

CHAPTER TEN

From the Flames

'We went through fire ... yet Thou hast brought us forth to a spacious place.' Psalm 66:12.

It was unusually quiet around Ibuno mission house on April 9 1907. Grace had finished a solitary midday meal and gone downstairs to attend to a patient in the dispensary. Sam had left that morning to help a young missionary mark out the site for a new mission house at Ikotobo, and the dispensary assistant had a day off.

Suddenly the stillness was shattered by a piercing shriek—

'The house is on fire! The house is on fire!'

Grace flew upstairs, to see smoke belching from the kitchen. Hard on her heels came David and other young men. Grabbing buckets they dashed to the water tank and tried frantically to quench the flames now gliding like fiery serpents between the roof and ceiling.

When it became clear that nothing could save the building, they turned their energies to pitching out anything that came to hand – chairs, bedding, food, books. Two boys stayed until the raging inferno cut off their access to the stairs. Climbing over the verandah they attempted to climb down the iron posts. One managed the 24-foot drop – but the other lost his grip and fell heavily on to the concrete floor, sustaining a spinal injury.

As Grace stood petrified, another small figure

appeared, silhouetted against the glow. A little girl, under treatment for a leg abscess, had been asleep on the floor of Etubom's room. In terror she scrambled over the verandah railing. Mrs. Bill could not bear to watch the inevitable disaster – but a gasp of amazement from the crowd of weeping Ibunos made her look up in time to see the child parachuting safely on to a pile of sand, the full skirt of her dress billowing out to break the fall.

Feeling suddenly faint, Grace put her hand to her head – and found it streaming with blood from an unnoticed injury. She stumbled towards the beach to bathe it and get away from the scene of destruction.

'Mma is going to drown herself,' cried the alarmed people. 'The shock has been too much for her.'

Then, seeing the wound, they led her gently away, laid her on a bed and brought water in a basin. Soon she was able to return to the smouldering ruins of her home. Two thoughts troubled her. Had she indirectly caused the fire by sending the kitchen boy on an errand? And how would poor Sam take the loss of this house, into which he had put so much careful planning and hard work? As she sat weeping on the steps of the church the women gathered round, exhorting: –

'Mma, remember Job! Remember Job! God will do the same for you.'

Then, making their way into the church, they besought the God of Job to bless Mma, and bring Etubom home safely and speedily.

One of David Ekong's first actions had been to dispatch an urgent message to Ikotobo. It was dark when the messengers arrived, but Sam set off immediately by bicycle, reaching the launch three hours later. By 4.30 a.m. he was home. He found Grace in better spirits than he had dared to hope during his long, anxious hours of travelling, being lovingly cared for by David and Mary in their own home.

Soon another visitor arrived, crippled with rheumatism and drenched with rain. It was Eka, a very old Christian woman, who had walked many miles to share their trouble. Putting her withered arms around them both she wept. Then, leaning on her stick, she blessed them and committed them to God's keeping. 'Her visit touched us more than anything,' they admitted later.

By this time it had been established that there had been no negligence in the kitchen, and that the fire must have originiated in the oven of the oil stove where bread was baking. Grace's other fear was relieved also, for far from depressing Sam the accident seemed to give him new energy.

Elder Ibok, now head of Egbo Egbo's family, had come at once to offer the use of the late chief's wood and iron house. Here the Bills gathered their few belongings and life began again. A week after the fire, Grace wrote:

'The Lord has been very merciful to us, for, although the things saved are scanty enough, they are the very things most needed and will make all the difference between a little comfort and absolute want.

'Anything like the kindness of the Christians I never saw. They have not ceased to bring us little gifts of cutlery, delph, household utensils and even personal attire. One woman brought me her wedding shoes and stockings, and another young fellow brought a pair of stockings, doubtless laid up for his marriage ... They have given us their best ... Our household goods are gone, but I think we can truly say "Thou has put gladness in our hearts more than in the time that their corn and their wine increased".'

Mrs. Bill was a born home-maker and, by May, her husband was reporting to his mother: 'Gracie still continues to make this little home improve. She has now got the hall covered with a piece of coco-matting that was saved from the fire. It looks very nice indeed, and feels very comfortable. We expect Mr. Weeks and our stores every day – every hour indeed – and Gracie has got the remaining room of this house ready to receive him. We are wondering what he will be like!'

The new missionary proved extremely useful in the big job that had to be tackled in coming months. The mission house which lay in ashes had been built in 1898, to replace the original one, then threatened by erosion of the riverbank. It was a three-storey building, after the style of the house in which Sam had spent his first few days at Calabar. The Ibunos expected the white man to build his home as high as possible, in an effort to rise above the intense humidity. Gracie's asthma had encouraged this policy. It also had the advantage of keeping all the personnel, and property, for which the missionary was responsible, under one sound roof.

In the Ibuno house each floor had a large central room. At ground level this formed a dining and class-room for the apprentices, with bedrooms opening from it to accommodate them, the houseboys and the dispensary boy. The first floor contained a big room for Bible classes and prayer meetings, together with the dispensary, store-room, and a room for strangers. The Bills lived on the second floor, which had a wide verandah supported by sixteen iron posts, and three bedrooms. One of these was often occupied by a patient needing special care. All this was now gone and the question arose – where, and to what plan, should the new house be built.?

About six miles north of Ibuno lay a narrow strip of land, formed by a loop in the river. Sam had often thought, as he steamed past, that it would make a fine site for a house. It was in Eket country, convenient to many villages with no Christian witness. Was this God's way of moving them to a more needy area? And might not this elevated site prove healthier for Grace? The more he thought and prayed, about it the more he was drawn to explore the possibilities. When the local chief offered the land freely no doubts remained in his mind. He would rebuild at Nditea – and the new house would have only two storeys – to save wear and tear on those varicose veins.

In the meantime, news of the fire had prompted friends at home to send gifts towards the project. Materials were dispatched, and in an improvised shack of rusty salvaged iron, with grocery boxes raised above the mud floor for beds, Samuel and Grace Bill, with George Weeks, set to work on the new mission station.

It was surely in answer to prayer that Grace's health allowed her to stay at her husband's side until building was complete, but in June 1908 she was carried once more aboard the home-bound steamer.

A year later Sam still on his own, was preparing to welcome a very special guest to Nditea. R. L. McKeown, now the Mission's general secretary, was coming back for a visit, and never was an arrival more eagerly anticipated. At the jetty 'Evangel' lay resplendent in a new coat of white paint. A couple of workboys with swinging machetes, cleared paths to the house, while two little girls washed the verandah floor. From the kitchen the aroma of freshly-baked bread wafted up to where Sam Bill was surveying his guest room with a critical eye.

Binding the rough edges of the coco-matting had been a tricky job, but the result was worthwhile and the carefully-laundered curtains hung crisply from their bamboo poles. The box which served as wash-stand did not please him. The only cover he could rake up was a faded blue flannel cloth snatched from the flames at Ibuno, but a clean white towel took the shabby look off it. As his eye caught a photograph on the bedside table,

82

The new house at Nditea.

he chuckled to himself. Wouldn't Mac be surprised to find a picture of his baby son waiting for him there!

The following weeks were exceedingly busy with mission and inter-mission business. Mr. McKeown was preparing to write a book to mark the Qua Iboe Mission's approaching twenty-fifth anniversary and as he travelled around the area with Mr. Bill he found ample evidence of church growth. At one place they were confronted by a group of boys.

'Will you please come?' they said. 'We want to show you a thing.'

Following through a maze of bush tracks they came to a clearing, in which stood a well-built church. Inside, everything was complete – seats, pulpit, and reading desk. More than thirty young people gathered round to press their claim.

'Two years pass by since we build this church. We

keep it fixed and ready, but no one has ever come. Oh, please send us a man to tell us about God!'

That scene was still vivid in the general secretary's memory when he completed his book 'Twenty-five Years in Qua Iboe.' He wrote:

'The appeal that led Mr. Bill to Ibuno in 1887 was faint when compared with the compelling call of today. Even fifteen years ago, nearly every town outside that tribe had its doors closed against the light. We then prayed for entrance . . . now we hear of a single section of the interior where six churches, still unoccupied, stand already built. God has taken us at our word, only His answer is so much greater than our prayers.

'The construction of railways and roads accentuates the urgency of the situation. Every kind of false teaching, and every form of sin, will now have access to the peoples of Southern Nigeria. The Moslems will reach them, and a godless civilization is already being carried among them by immoral Europeans. Meanwhile the little churches are rotting in the rain . . .'

Just before Mac's departure, Sam took him to see old Eka, now very frail and longing for Home. She had heard that the visitor brought with him from Ireland, news of the death of Etubom Bill's mother.

'I will see her soon,' she affirmed happily.

'Yes,' Sam agreed. 'And what great talks you will have together!'

Although they had never met on earth, he knew the two women would have much in common. Life had brought many trials to them, but each had found strength in her God. For over twenty years both had followed every development in Qua Iboe with faith and prayer. Both women loved and cared for him and his family. It was easy to picture them together, in the presence of their Lord.

CHAPTER ELEVEN

The Small Ones

'Take heed that ye despise not one of these little ones.'
Matt. 18:10.

Samuel Bill took one look in his bedroom mirror – and began to laugh.

'Boy, that'll teach you to tempt providence,' he told himself.

He certainly cut a comical figure, in pyjama coat, trousers several sizes too large, and borrowed boots. And all because he had wanted to please Gracie.

Three weeks earlier he had said goodbye to her at Belfast dock and embarked on S.S. Nigeria – a vessel renowned as the meeting place of Mr. Joe Chamberlain, Lord Roberts and Lord Kitchener with the Boer generals. The purser on board was an old friend, with a common interest in motor-boats. Sam got some useful hints from him, and read a few good books loaned by a fellow passenger but, what with noisy drinking and roulette parties and having to share a small cabin with a young fellow 'very nervous about himself' he found the voyage exceedingly tedious. 'I wish I could fall asleep and not waken again till we get to Calabar,' was his comment.

Having promised Grace to appear at Eket in 'decent garb' he set off on the last lap of the journey, attired in brand-new lustre jacket, stiff collar and shirt front. It was June, and the rains had begun with a vengeance.

By the time he had cycled to Eket he was 'like a drowned rat'. Instead of making a good impression, he had to submit to the indignity of borrowed garments, topped by a pyjama jacket extricated from his hand luggage. Truth to tell it was a relief to get out of the starched collar – and at least he had tried to keep his word.

Now he was back at Nditea, with scores of familiar faces waiting to greet him. A number of children were obviously keen to be chosen for house-helpers, among them a little one called Grace. That name could not be refused, and another girl about the same age was selected to keep her company.

The house-children had different duties. One looked after the pantry and another kept the rooms clean. A boy would do the washing, while another cooked food on the wood-burning stove. Then there were work boys for the launch, and for general maintenance and repair jobs. When all the chores were finished, Etubom would call out 'Come on children, time for a dip!' and off they trooped to dive and swim, to splash and frolic in the river that was as much their element as dry land.

Every day the youngsters had school lessons on the verandah and, morning and evening, they gathered for family prayers. After dark, when the meal was over and Mr. Bill busy with his books, they would sit round the big table playing Snap, draughts or snakes and ladders. He loved to listen to their cheerful chatter, to watch their faces glow with excitement in the lamp-light, and then to hear young voices singing the hymns of his own childhood.

There were tears as well as smiles for the small ones. For all her eagerness to live at Nditea, little Grace grew homesick. Etubom noticed her dullness.

'What's wrong, Grace?' he asked with a kindly hand on her shoulder.

Big tears trickled down the brown cheeks as she replied 'Please, Etubom, I had a bad dream last night. I dreamed that my mother was dead.'

'Dearie me,' said he. 'That's terrible. But if anything like that happened they would send us word at once. I tell you what, next time the canoe is going to Ibuno you'll go home and see for yourself that she's all right. Come on now and I'll give you a ride on my bicycle.'

Tears and fears forgotten, the child went off for her favourite treat, and when the canoe next left for Ibuno she wouldn't go – without Etubom.

Samuel Bill knew how to deal wisely with youthful misdemeanours.

'The best boys have a rough side,' he'd say, adding significantly, 'I suppose we each find the side we pull uppermost!'

On one occasion the precious sugar was disappearing uncommonly quickly. Calling all the boys together he announced a reward of six manillas (just over sixpence) to anyone who could answer a simple question. The offer produced great delight, the pantry boy in particular dancing with glee.

'Can any boy tell why it is that a tin of sugar, kept in the pantry, lasts only three and a half days – while the same tin, kept in the house, lasts seven days?'

There was a sudden silence – and the pantry boy's face told its own tale. Etubom said no more, but in a prayer meeting, soon afterwards, a subdued voice was heard to say:

'Lord, please make me a good boy.'

Another day, returning unexpectedly, Mr. Bill found a girl stealing manillas. These horse-shoe shaped pieces of iron formed the local currency, and were kept in heavy boxes awaiting transport to Eket. Usually they were under lock and key, for it wasn't fair to put temptation in the way of small hands. But there were always opportunities if a child had a mind to steal. The girl burst into tears.

On the face of it she should be dismissed, but what would become of her then? The best thing would be to send for her father, and let him punish her. Next day the father arrived, ignorant of what had happened and in excellent spirits.

'He was in such good form I couldn't bear to tell him, knowing the Ibunos think so badly of it,' Sam confessed when reporting the incident to his wife. 'So I gave her a good warning and hope she will mend her ways. You remember U.........? Well so far as I know she never stole again.'

About this time a lively newcomer joined the household. A missionary going on furlough didn't know what to do with his pet monkey and, remembering Mr. Bill's fondness for the creature, suggested he might keep it. Before long the two were inseparable. Sitting or walking, the monkey would perch on his shoulder, till he became almost unaware of its presence. One day they were on the way to Eket before he remembered it was there; on another occasion the little animal clung to him tenaciously while he dived and swam in the river!

Several monkeys came and went in the Bill household over the years. One played havoc with Grace's treasured lace curtains and caused such heartache that Sam was forced to get rid of him, but a diary note reveals how hard it was to do the deed: 'I think the little fellow never knew a thing about it. He was asleep in his box, and I emptied the stuff on a piece of lint I had put there before he went in. He just went on sleeping until he died. He was lying on his side in the box in the morning.

I could not sleep all night after it, and felt quite sick in the morning. He was a dear little pet.'

Perhaps it was the mischievous streak in Sam Bill's nature that gave him such an affection for his monkeys. Perhaps the same trait, combined with a humble, child-like spirit made him such a favourite with children. But, above all, it was the love of his Master for little ones that drew them together, as steel to a magnet.

Wherever Samuel Bill went he was accompanied by a crowd of youngsters. They would gather on the beach, ready at the least invitation to pile into the launch. At every destination others would be waiting, to carry his belongings and tell him the latest news. In Ibuno, there wasn't a child whom he did not know. Many of them he had helped to bring into the world, and when they were sick he was their doctor. It gave him great satis-faction to see them growing up healthy and happy, learning the stories of Jesus and able to read His Word.

On Sunday afternoons, wherever Etubom happened to be, 'the small ones' took over. He always had picture books for them to look at and never seemed weary of their questions. Time and again he would report to Gracie:

'About thirty boys here this afternoon – eighty children altogether. All want to see the photo of Ibuno (Jack).

'The house is shaking with all the running – the place is full all the time. This is the best time I have had.'

Although living at Nditea, Mr. Bill loved Ibuno, and decided to build himself a little rest house there. When it was nearing completion he wrote:

'I have had a great afternoon. Up till the time the school bell rang the house was filled with children . . . All are delighted that the house is built and all march about as if it belonged to them! If the house was finished, well, I think I will be often there.'

Not everyone could tolerate such invasions. Samuel Bill did not expect all homes to welcome swarms of children but, like his Master, he sternly rebuked any attempt to drive them away.

Visiting a new missionary couple one day he heard the wife chasing two children, who were clinging with dirty hands to freshly-painted rails in order to get a peep at the visitor. Boiling with indignation he went after the little ones, brought them indoors, and spent the rest of his visit with one on each knee. 'I can stand most things but not that,' he wrote to Grace. A missionary was in Africa to bring Christ to the people. If she had no love for them, nor they for her, she might as well go home.

Samuel Bill's popularity was not limited to African children. He was equally at home with the junior members of missionary families. Visiting a Church of Scotland doctor, he was introduced briefly to the tiny daughter of the house. Eighteen months later, when the family came to stay at Nditea, Sam wondered if Maimie would remember him. He was soon left without doubt. 'She ran to me and gave me a kiss,' he reported to Gracie. 'She's a great little girl.'

While her mother took charge of the cooking, Maimie spent her time with Grandpa Bill. He had planned some special treats – a picnic under the trees at Big Town and an afternoon's fun with the house-children, in the breakers at 'the point'. Then, tired and happy, he wrote:

'Maimie has been sitting all the evening with me, on my couch, till her mother took her off to bed.'

Through the love of many children Samuel Bill was compensated, in some measure, for long separations from his own daughter and son. It was never easy to leave those two forlorn little figures on the quayside when the parents embarked for another term in Nigeria. The children were well cared for by grandparents and teacher-aunt in Belfast, and were often joined by their mother when her health broke down, but their father had little opportunity to enjoy their company.

Sometimes, when Grace was in Qua Iboe, they hid their heartache by arranging a little party to celebrate the birthday of Emma or Jack, thousands of miles away in Ireland. One October 28, after a feast and games for the house-children and the Ekong family, Sam wrote a poignant note in his diary, 'It just wanted Emma here to finish the thing.'

Christmas was another time when separation was hard to bear, but the Bills gave no place to self-pity and threw themselves, heart and soul, into planning a happy day for the small ones within their reach. There were races and games for all the schoolchildren, and each one received a little present ordered months previously from home – a gay handkerchief, a pencil or perhaps a comb, to be treasured for years to come.

The giving was not one-sided. One Christmas morning Sam and Grace Bill were getting ready for the service, when their two house-girls appeared at the door.

'Well, what do you want?'

'Etubom, when the ladies stayed here last month they dashed us this money.'

In the pink palm of each brown hand lay two precious six-pences.

'Please Etubom' they continued, 'could you change these into shillings for us to give in the offering today?'

The church, decorated with palm fronds, was packed to capacity, with children crowding up the pulpit steps; the singing was hearty and the Word was sweet. But the memory to linger with the missionaries was of two small girls, saving all that they had, to give to the Christ-child on His Birthday.

CHAPTER TWELVE

God's Plan Still Stands

'It fell not, for it was founded upon a rock.' Matt
7:25.

The wharf at Eket was buzzing with conversation
when Sam Bill arrived to collect his supplies, and the
latest world news.

'Any word about the Home Rule moves for Ireland?'
he enquired from the agent.

'No, but there's a serious situation in Europe' he
was told. 'War has broken out between Germany and
Prussia. Before long the whole of Europe may be into
it.'

'That's bad. How will it affect the steamer?'

'Nobody can tell. With the Germans in control of
the Cameroons there may be activity in this area.'

A chill wind made Sam Bill shiver as he set off for
home. There had been a queer spell of weather, no
rain for over three weeks, with temperatures as low as
67° in the mornings, and a constant cool breeze. Old
folk could remember no rainy season like it, and they
watched fearfully as crops withered before their eyes.
It was treacherous for people with no warm clothing.
Even the white man, in his flannel shirt, had caught a
chill from which he was just recovering. But it wasn't
only the temperature that made him shiver that August
day in 1914.

Six months previously, before saying goodbye to

Grace, and leaving Ireland for another term of service, he had written a farewell message for readers of the Mission magazine. It radiated a confidence that would be severely tested before he saw Belfast again.

'During the past year our work has been full of encouragement. The promise "Lo, I am with you alway" has been richly fulfilled to us, and the presence of the Chief Worker is evidenced in many ways. No other year witnessed such an accession of members, over 560 having been received in the different churches, and the number of African workers – over 70 – added to our staff has surpassed all previous years. Not only so, but the liberality of the people has abounded beyond our most sanguine expectations, over £3,000 having been given by them towards the spread of the Gospel and the education of the young.

'Besides all this, the Lord of the harvest has been exercising His prerogative and four European workers have already gone out to give much needed help. Four others have been accepted and are going shortly. Two of these latter are teachers, for whom many of our friends have been praying. With their aid, and that of a friend who has undertaken the cost of the building, we hope to have our higher school under way in the near future, and our ability for training correspondingly increased.

'Our organisation in Qua Iboe is being perfected. Ask for us that we may have wisdom to shape its growth in accordance with the teaching that is from Above; and, most important of all, that the Church which is growing up may be one that is full of spiritual life and power, and that every member of it may seek to live and walk with Jesus, and be indwelt by His Spirit.'

Two of the new recruits travelled out with the returning founder on board S.S. Nigeria. They had settled in well during the intervening months, Tom Gamble busy in the workshop at Nditea and Tom Fettis completing the rest house at Ibuno. Plans were in hand for a fine new church, for which much material had accompanied them from Britain, and Sam was in his element, designing, demonstrating, transporting and supervising.

He was pleased with the young men. They weren't afraid of hard work; they got on well with the people; they were easy to live with, and they shared his spiritual aims. The only snag was that neither of them liked palm oil chop! It was well for him that he enjoyed local food, for imported supplies grew scarce as German U-boats became active. At one stage Fettis and Gamble were reduced to a diet of trade biscuits, the former complaining that his jaws were always tired before his stomach was satisfied!

At home, fears were being expressed that the mission income would suffer, but Sam remained convinced that no enemy action could obstruct God's supply line.

'If we are in earnest about getting the work done that He has given us He will see that our needs are all met. And I don't think there are any laggards among our number. Everyone is busy at his particular job, whether it is superintending out-stations, instructing teachers or building.'

'A little incident may interest you,' he continued. 'Before the last supplies reached us the chop store at Nditea had run very low, and for about three weeks the beef tins were finished. During that time fish was constantly offered for sale, so that the workers always had a meal. Since the steamer arrived, these supplies of fish have ceased. Although we live in a fishing district fish is very seldom sold as people prefer to dry it.'

That year there was no flour to make bread for the Communion service, and no sugar for the wine. But if the symbols were absent, the reality was present, and Etubom's two house-girls were among the record number of 123 new believers who took their place around the Lord's Table.

The war dragged on. By 1916 Gracie's health had improved enough to allow her to rejoin her husband. It wasn't easy to leave Ireland. She had been helping in the Sandes' Soldiers' Home at Ballykinlar, and her heart went out to the boys passing through on their way to France. As she laughed at their pranks and listened to their problems, she was thinking of her own dear lad, and his offer of service even then under consideration. A weak leg might exempt him from active service – it depended how great the need for recruits. She wouldn't have wanted to hold him back, but she couldn't bear the thought of his taking the lives of others – not her gentle, sensitive Jack. Now he was in the Royal Army Medical Corps, and Emma was engaged in teaching and part-time V.A.D. work in England. There was nothing to hold Grace in Ireland, and she was needed at her husband's side.

It had been a nerve-racking voyage. On the first Sunday night she had a strong sense of danger, and cried to the Lord for protection.

'I have heard their cry and am come down to deliver them,' was the word that came, with great assurance.

Some days later, in conversation with the first officer, she related her experience. He was silent for a moment and then said quietly:

'There *was* something happening that night. For hours we were followed by a vessel, which crossed and recrossed our path, and then followed, hiding her lights. No friendly captain would have done that.'

So when the Ibuno Christians gathered to give thanks for her safe arrival Grace was able to tell them:

'Dear friends, God did hear your prayers and brought us safely through.'

The following weekend brought communion Sunday. Pastor David's ministry was always inspiring to Samuel and Grace Bill, but never more so than that day. He based his sermon on the notice board beside the little railway which ran up the hill at Calabar. 'STAND! LISTEN! LOOK!' it read. With deep feeling Pastor Ekong drew his hearers to stand, listen, and look at the foot of the cross.

'Lord Jesus, why did you allow them to bind your hands with cords like that?'

'Because you were bound in the slavery of sin, by fetters far stronger than these. You could never break them but, by My being bound, you are made free.'

'And those blood-marks on your back – the marks of the cruel lash – why those, Lord Jesus? Thieves and wicked men are beaten so, but You – the Holy Sinless One, why have *You* been beaten?'

'I have been beaten for the broken laws of God, which you have violated. I kept them all, but you sinners have broken them all. I am beaten for your sins, and by My stripes you are healed.'

'Why did You not clear Yourself, Lord Jesus?'

'Because had I cleared Myself, I should have condemned you . . . Only by My silence could I justify you.'

'Look – at Gethsemane and see what *sin* cost Him. Our daily toil costs us sweat of water, but so awful was the work He had to do, that it wrung great drops of blood from His body. Look – and fear to sin – because of what sin meant to Jesus.'

'The Lord was very near us as David spoke,' wrote Grace Bill. 'One could see by people's faces how the Word was going home.'

Soon afterwards, word came that Jack had received

his commission, and been posted to France with the Royal Irish Rifles. Grace longed to get home to see him once more before he faced the firing line, but her hopes were dashed by rumours that no women passengers were allowed to travel. Letters were slow in coming. Three or four weeks might pass without news, and the suspense was harrowing. Out-going mails were equally uncertain, but mother and father kept writing long, loving letters, with details of the work in which they prayed their son might be spared to join them.

On July 3 a cable came to say that Jack's regiment had left for France. His parents were at Ibuno for the funeral of an elder. Sam almost broke down as he took part in the service, and afterwards had to go to bed with one of his bad atttacks of fever, accompanied by severe head and back pains.

That evening Grace sat writing to her son: 'It is a glorious moonlight night and away to the right of the moon, the two pointers of the Southern Cross are shining brightly. Isn't it wonderful – those two lovely stars always pointing to the Cross, so that when you see the one you see the other? What a lesson for us!

'David gave a lovely thought in his sermon on Sunday – Jesus is the Vine, we are the branches. The parent stem bears no fruit – that is all found on the branches. So, Jesus looks to us to bear fruit for Him. He was speaking of the parable of the trees wanting a king, and how the vine, olive, and fig all refused. "They knew the work God wanted them to do and they were determined to do it." He exhorted us so earnestly to *cultivate and use* whatever gift God has given us.

'While I have been writing the moon has suddenly darkened. At first the lower half seemed filled with a brownish-red substance – then almost covered, and now there seems like a great dark mass in it – most strange. Father thinks it is an eclipse . . . I took Father's field glasses and went out again and it looks lovely now – a great darkish, amber-coloured globe, and, suspended in its centre, a big black ball. I wonder will you see it' . . .

Next morning Grace continued:

'Morning July 5. It *was* an eclipse of the moon. Before I went to bed nearly half was clear, and the big, black ball was going out at the top corner like a huge mountain. I suppose the atmospheric conditions here, especially at this season, account for the strange colours we saw . . . A lot of people gathered to David's house – one man in particular wanted to be near him if anything happened. Alas, when *that* day comes we shall be unable to help.

'Mary asked me to tell you that all the people are praying for you. If you could see their faces as they look at your photo and then say, "O Abasi, kama eyen oro ono nyin, O Obong, fuk enye ke mba fo." – "God keep that child for us. O Lord, cover him with Thy feathers." '

On the first Friday in October the Bills were preparing to go to Ibuno for another Communion weekend. The launch was packed with supplies and Sam already in it when a messenger arrived with an unsealed envelope. Opening it hastily, Grace found the cable – '2nd Lieut. John Bill, 12th R.I.R. – MISSING.'

The word 'MISSING' struck like a sword to the mother's heart. At the beach Sam heard the piercing cry and knew the worst had happened.

It was a devastating blow. Jack was a handsome, gifted lad and a true Christian. His parents had been saving for years in order that he might study medicine and eventually join the Mission as a qualified doctor. Often, as his father patched up a broken body, he had looked forward to the day when his son would do a better job; now he could only write in his diary – 'The pride of our life has gone out and the hope of our life is laid low.'

Grace was inconsolable. Jack and she had been extremely close in temperament and understanding. Already weakened by typhoid fever, she was in no fit state to bear the shock, and in the midst of his own grief Sam was deeply concerned for her welfare. All efforts to comfort her seemed of no avail, so, slipping away quietly on his own, he sobbed out his heartache and problem to his Heavenly Father. Would He please comfort Gracie as He saw her nature needed?

The first solace came with the arrival of a young missionary for the week-end. 'His prayer was like Jack's, so simple and earnest. It seemed to loosen the band round my heart and I was able to pray too,' she recalled later.

Reassurance came also with an awareness of her son's nearness. 'I have seen no form, I hear nothing with my earthly ears, but I hear his dear voice in my heart and I believe what he said, "God sent me to comfort you".'

On Sunday the stricken parents received strength to attend the Communion service and join in the singing of Jack's favourite hymn, 'I gave My life for thee.' Grace wrote to Emma, 'The oldest elder, Ibok, prayed a lovely prayer. He told the Lord that although they were black and we were white, their feelings were the same as ours. Sorrow touched them as it touched us. He begged God to comfort us, for although their hearts were so sore, they could do nothing.'

Sympathy flowed around them from all quarters; even the old captain on the passing steamer lowered the Union Jack to half-mast and stood with bowed head as he neared Ibuno. He too had lost a son, on a torpedoed ship.

Normally it would have taken a letter almost a month to follow the cable with details of Jack's death, but

'God was mercifulness itself to us. The cable was delayed in some way and so we got the details just three days afterwards.' It was Grace who managed to read aloud the account of the action in which their son lost his life – 'leading his men like a gallant officer.'

In spite of his sense of inadequacy, Samuel Bill himself did more than anyone to help his wife, as she told their daughter, separated from them by thousands of miles – 'No one else could have comforted me as he has done. . . . His faith is grand and he believes that, though *our plans* are broken, God's have been fulfilled.'

The same triumphant spirit was evident in Mr. Bill's letter to R. L. McKeown: 'The Lord Himself undertook for us in a wonderful way. He has taken all the sting away and given us the assurance most real and deep that He has done the very best. Our comfort is that God's Plan still stands. The service Jack and we hoped he should render here is being given Above. This experience is something we shall treasure in our hearts, and thank God for, all our lives.'

CHAPTER THIRTEEN

The Work Force

'For we are labourers together with God.' *1 Cor. 3:9.*

'O Obong, afo edi ebiet idung nyin ke ofuri emana.' –
'Lord, Thou hast been our dwelling place in all
generations.'

Samuel Bill's Efik was a bit rusty, but inspiration
came from two hundred happy faces, beaming their
welcome at the Ibuno prayer meeting. He was delighted
to be back again after a furlough which had been ex-
tended to ten months by serious illness, and vein surgery
in March 1918.

Christmas Day had been spent on the steamer lying
off Calabar. Two days later he had cycled to the mission
house at Ikotobo, where Will Eakin briefed him on the
latest news. The virulent epidemic of influenza which
swept Europe in the last days of war had claimed many
victims in West Africa. Reports at the various ports of
call had raised his fears for the safety of missionaries
and church leaders. Mercifully, all these had escaped,
but hundreds of deaths had taken place in Qua Iboe,
and 'the Big Disease' was still rampant in some areas.
All missionaries were well and working happily together.
'That,' he confessed, 'was the best hearing I have had
for a long time'.

The date of Etubom's arrival had been uncertain, but
the news spread like wildfire. His reception at Nditea
was described in a letter to Grace:

'When I got to the corner at Etia's house the first one to see me was the little girl who is always nursing the big baby. She gave a great shout and ran and hugged me. Then out came Etia and Asuqua, the witchdoctor next door. I was nearly smothered!

'Etia took my arm and linked me right up into the house. There were great "Mbom – Os" ("Alas") when they found out you were not with me, but they were a little mollified when I said you were coming in a few months. Before I was long in the house I think the whole village had come.

'Etia killed a fowl and made me palm oil chop and fufu and fish black soup. So I had a great dinner. All afternoon and evening we had a great time talking about many things, and then we had a time of prayer. . . . The house seemed full of you – and yet you were not here.'

The New Year was only a few days old when an urgent message arrived – 'Eakin is ill in the rest house at Atabong.' The launch was not yet in going order, so Sam set off by canoe. Recognising the urgency of the situation he dispatched an SOS to the Church of Scotland doctor. He too was handicapped by lack of transport, but started out immediately to cover the 54 miles by pedal bicycle. Arriving exhausted, he confirmed the diagnosis. The patient seemed too ill to move, but his only hope of survival lay in surgery. Providentially, a trader's car was going to where a launch could be obtained for the last part of the journey.

Sam Bill waited anxiously for news at the Eket Post Office. It was his fifty-fifth birthday. He saw good value in socks at the store and bought six pairs – but his thoughts and prayers were in Calabar hospital. The first telegram read, 'Operation performed last night. Abscess found. Condition serious.' Another in similar vein arrived next morning. The third bore news of Eakin's death after a second operation.

A few months later Samuel Bill was in Calabar to meet his wife and daughter at the steamer. It was Jack's death that had finally decided Emma to offer for service in Qua Iboe. She could never take her brother's place as a doctor, but she had some nursing experience and was qualified to teach music. Her application was welcomed, not only because of her suitability as a missionary, but also for the support she could give her ageing parents. In Belfast at the end of March, Emma and three other young women had taken part in a memorable farewell meeting at which her mother gave the closing address. For years Grace Bill had been pleading for more help for the women and girls of Qua Iboe. Now, after crushing sorrow, her prayers were being answered and as she spoke that night, few eyes were dry or hearts unmoved.

Before the final stage of their journey, Samuel Bill and his daughter paid a visit to the quiet cemetery at Calabar, and stood beside a simple headstone bearing the inscription – 'W. C. Eakin, died 13th January, 1919.'

'How many years had he in Qua Iboe?' the girl asked.

'Fifteen,' replied her father. 'I attended his farewell service when I was on furlough in 1904.'

'You wrote home that he just seemed to have found his nîche and never knew what it was to be lonely,' she recalled.

'Aye, it's hard to know why such a useful worker should be taken so young. But then there's a lot we'll not understand till we get up yonder.'

Turning to the next grave he shook his head sadly.

'I feel just as badly about that poor doctor. Little did I think when he cycled all those miles in the heat of the day that he was ill himself and would be gone a few days after Eakin. He was one of the nicest men I ever met.'

Father and daughter were facing afresh the cost of obedience to God's call, for Will Eakin was the fourth Qua Iboe missionary to be laid to rest in African soil, and many more had been invalided home with no hope of return.

'But we don't all die young.'

Sam Bill broke the silence, pointing with a smile to the nearby memorial to the renowned Mary Slessor.

'The last time I saw that old lady she was as brisk as a bee, riding ahead on her bicycle to direct us on our way after a conference. Maybe you'll be like her, Emma.'

There was no concealing his pleasure at having his daughter in Africa once again.

Emma was designated to teach in the Girls' Institute at Eket, but first she must see Nditea and revisit her birthplace. The Ibunos still regarded her as one of their own children and proudly showed her around the new church, school, dispensary and workshops.

'See what a great work your father has done!' they exclaimed.

Soon she was immersed in her own duties while her parents carried on with theirs, but the many essential trips to Eket held a new attraction and, in turn, Emma loved to get down-river for a few days or hours of relaxation.

Once the Bills were sitting after dark in an out-station rest house when they heard the tinkle of a bicycle bell.

'What's that?'

Grace's startled question was answered by suppressed laughter and the singing of 'Tipperary' outside the door. Two girlish figures appeared, hot and thirsty after a stiff ride from Eket. Emma and a fellow-teacher had decided to give her parents a surprise. After years of separation it was comforting to be within reach of each other once more.

Samuel Bill rarely complained about his health but he was by no means immune from the effects of a tropical climate, hard work and advancing years. Often his diary records – 'A splitting headache today,' 'Rheumatism bad,' or 'Down with fever.' It was in 1920 that a doctor, examining Grace, insisted on checking up on her husband. He discovered a faulty valve in his heart and ordered complete rest. The prescription was followed for a day! After that he tried to avoid the heaviest manual tasks, but continued with virtually everything else.

Although most of the missionaries had some practical skills, it was to Father Bill that they brought their motor bicycles for major repairs and overhaul, as did also some of the Europeans at Eket and of course there were always his own engines to be kept in running order. A friend had given him a small motorboat which was handy and economical for short trips, but the launch was still essential for freight. It was now powered by an outboard motor, the bodywork being built and rebuilt as time and tide took toll of its fabric.

Writing to her friend Mrs. McKeown, Grace described her husband's typical attitude to difficulties: 'Boat-building is heavy work, and of course it is over and above the rest of his work. Fancy, Mary, every nail hole in the boat has to be bored – and he has done most of that himself. The wood is awfully hard and all his "bits" got broken, but was *Sam* downhearted?!! *Not a bit*! He got the ribs out of an old umbrella and made new ones galore – and even some out of knitting pins. The workshop is very draughty and he has got rheumatism in both shoulders – but he won't have them rubbed!!!'

The end of hostilities in 1918 found the Qua Iboe Mission, in common with societies all over the world, in urgent need of male recruits. A survey of unoccupied territories to the west and north resulted in the following statement in the mission magazine: 'To maintain the existing work and to enter these territories, at least eight new men are needed. The Empire counted no sacrifice too great – giving its noblest to win through in the fearful struggle of the past four years. The voice of One who has redeemed the world speaks to us, through the confusion of war's sad aftermath, of His unfinished work.'

A year later the four young women had been accepted but still – 'The need for men becomes more and more urgent ... we earnestly request our friends to pray for the eight new workers, for whom we have been appealing for over a year.'

Unknown to those who prayed, the call was already sounding in the hearts of young men in England, Ireland, and Scotland, and by August 1922 the last of this 'post-war eight' was on his way to Africa. His first encounter with the Founder took place at Eket, where Mr. Bill had come to meet him. Youthful Scot and greybearded Ulsterman eyed each other keenly, and liked what they saw. Leaping nimbly into the launch the older man remarked with a twinkle,

'Not bad for a man whose heart is hanging by a thread, eh?'

Once aboard, he whipped off collar and tie, opened the neck of his flannel shirt and breathed a sigh of relief.

'I only put it on to please the wife,' he admitted. 'She likes me to look presentable when I meet those white people at Eket.'

It was an education to spend a few days in the Bill

household, and the guest soon discovered that his host was quietly sizing him up.

'How would you tackle this?' asked Mr. Bill, holding with the tongs a bar of iron, red-hot from the furnace. The former ship-yard welder considered the metal and suggested how best to obtain the required angle.

'I see you know a thing or two,' was the satisfied comment.

The next test was more daunting, even for an ex-R.A.M.C. man who had dealt with front-line casualties in France. A fourteen-year-old boy had been bitten on the foot by a snake and by the time he was brought to Mr. Bill, the leg had become gangrenous. What should he do? Remembering the resourceful young missionary, now in his own station at Mbiuto, he dispatched the patient and his friends there with a note.

When the little company arrived, Herbert Dickson opened the letter and stood aghast at its contents. The writer suggested that, if he could amputate the leg at the knee, the boy's life might be saved. He *couldn't* do it. It was outrageous to suggest such a thing. But if nothing was done, the boy would surely die – and what would Mr. Bill think of him then? There was nothing for it but to roll up his sleeves, scrub up, and somehow get on with the job. By God's help the operation was successful, and Samuel Bill was confirmed in his estimate of the latest recruit, whose service was to span the next half century.

The Founder of the Qua Iboe Mission rarely used the word 'missionary'. He preferred 'worker'. For one thing it applied equally to black or white, and for another it indicated the right attitude of mind. He was a shrewd judge of character, and derived great satisfaction from seeing a new member fitting happily into the team.

'If a man is to do his best work,' he once wrote, 'it must be with a congenial fellow-worker, and in congenial surroundings, otherwise worry will impair his spirit and his health.'

In a small Mission it was not always easy to achieve this ideal. Not every 'round peg' found a 'round hole' – but a change of location could work wonders – so long as he was 'a godly, earnest man who tries to do his work as unto the Lord.' That was the one indispensable qualification.

CHAPTER FOURTEEN

The Growing Church

'From you sounded out the Word of the Lord.' 1 Thess.
1:8.

'Sam, don't forget to tell me when we get near the
bridge.' The plaintive voice came from behind a huge
pile of luggage, stacked high on the sidecar.

The rider of the motor-bike chuckled.

'We're over it long ago,' he replied.

'But Sam, you never slowed down.'

'What's the sense of slowing down,' he reasoned.
'Sure the quicker you get over it the better.'

It suited Samuel Bill very well to have his wife's
view limited by the carefully-balanced loads. True, she
could hear the squawks of the chickens and bleating of
goats, making for cover at the approach of the unfamiliar
machine, but if he was able to get a good straight run
at the bridges without her knowledge, they were both
saved the panic that still seized her at the sight of those
precarious planks.

Her fears were not without foundation. Once she
had been in the sidecar, with a boy riding pillion behind
her husband, when the whole lot went overboard. Sam's
back was strained but, considering everything, they had
a 'wonderful escape.' Thirty years earlier Grace had
been almost drowned when a canoe capsized near Etinan
beach. Three times she had gone under and would
certainly have been lost, but for the prompt action of

an apprentice who dived to the rescue. It was many months before she dared venture into a canoe again – and never without trepidation.

The motor-bike was Samuel Bill's latest acquisition, and, after years of frustratingly slow travel, it was sheer bliss to speed along at thirty miles an hour. The entire area was intersected by creeks and stretches of swamp. Only a few of the primitive log bridges could be attempted by even the most daring cyclist, but an element of risk added zest to Sam's expeditions. His passengers did not always share his enthusiasm. Slithering through mud, or choking with dry-season dust was not everyone's idea of pleasure. Many a new arrival had his first big test of faith on the pillion seat or sidecar of the founder's motor-bike!

When Grace was well enough to accompany her husband, she willingly put up with the hazards of travel for the pleasure of visiting her friends. As he conducted his business she would share the problems of the missionary wives and local women, often gaining insights denied to others and offering helpful advice. Best of all she loved to go to one of the out-stations, living among the people in the little rest house reserved by them for their guests. Describing a typical visit to Afaha Eket, she wrote:

'The mud house had been nicely prepared. Walls and floors remudded, a small stand with a wash-hand basin, two native beds and three long bamboo seats, also two small tables, large pots of water and plenty of firewood had been provided.

'On Sunday morning the church was crowded – about 600 – and over 80 remembered the Lord's death. Mr. Bill preached from "My Son, give Me Thine heart" – in Efik of course – and they listened earnestly. I never was followed by such a crowd as that which accompanied us from church – fully 100 – right, left, back and front

Ibuno Fishing Canoe.

– boys, girls, and young people! They followed us right into the house, and from then till 6 o'clock there was a throng!

'Several sick people came too – and one childless woman, whom we treated last time, brought a lovely baby boy in her market basket, to show us what God had done for her and to ask me to pray that the child may live. They are not Christians yet, but she promised to go to church and learn "God's fashion". It may be that "A little child shall lead them".'

The Bills had great compassion and understanding for childless couples who came to them for help. On this visit they had another reminder of the problem. 'A nice looking woman, a Christian who is childless, was put out of her home some time ago. Her husband is also a member of the church – but this is too hard a test for his Christianity, and so he is seeking another wife. At her request Mr. Bill heard the palaver . . . but although she said she would go back, and be a good wife, her husband would not agree. Her sorrowful face made our hearts sore for her as we came away.

'Very, very few can stand this test. They love children, and marriage without them is, to their minds, an absolute failure. In fact the way in which they regard children is proving a very serious drawback to the work at present. Lots of the Christian girls came to see us, fine, loving-hearted girls who might be a great power for God if only they are kept from evil. I spoke a few earnest words to them before leaving, urging upon them how the heart of Jesus is grieved when His Name is dishonoured.'

Sometimes the visit involved a longer journey to places like Iko. Samuel Bill had been there many times to conduct communion services, ordain elders and help in the building of their church. This was Gracie's first visit – indeed the first visit of any white woman – and there was great excitement when word got around that she was on the way.

An early start had been needed to catch the right tide for crossing the bar, so pots and pans, beds and bedding, drugs and food were all aboard 'Evangel' before daylight. All that was forgotten was Etubom's pyjamas! The journey took four hours, down the clear river to the open sea, along the muddy coastal waters, and then inland again through a mass of creeks.

'Oh look Sam, the biggest crocs I've ever seen,' exclaimed Gracie, pointing to the mud flats, where two enormous crocodiles lay – near enough for a spine-chilling view of cavernous jaws and wicked eyes. In the overhanging branches, draped with tropical creepers, big and little black monkeys with white fringe whiskers leapt and chattered. Humid heat closed in upon the travellers as they steamed further inland and there before them, on a long ridge of ground, was Iko.

It was a quaint spot, with grass-roofed mud houses very closely packed together to accommodate about a thousand inhabitants. 'Just like a typical picture of an African village,' thought Grace.

She loved the place from the start, and enjoyed every minute of their week's stay. While Sam was busy with the fine young teacher and three newly-ordained elders, she had a constant stream of callers. Children, adorable and very friendly, swarmed around in dozens. The women were more timid at first.

'Mma, please Mma.' A venturesome hand gently touched Grace's head. She knew what was wanted by the group of wide-eyed women and smiled reassuringly. Taking the pins from her hair, she let it fall, dark and shining, about her slender shoulders, to be greeted by gasps of amazement. Once she would have shrunk from such a public display, but not now. This was the sixth time to-day, and she was glad to do it – for Jesus' sake.

As Mr. and Mrs. Bill joined in the Communion service that Sunday in Iko, they were thinking back to 1899, and their decision to release Abasi Mfon from the Ibuno dispensary to go to Okorotip. For several years the going had proved tough in that low-lying swampy place whose inhabitants were plagued with fever and rheumatism, but gradually they began to see the benefits of Abasi's medical care, and to heed his faithful preaching.

It was amazing to witness the transformation of a whole community. The location of the town was moved to slightly higher ground. Leaky grass huts gave place to neat houses, on raised foundations of clay brought down-river by canoe. Red earthen walls and brown mat roofs blended harmoniously with the dark green background of mangrove trees. The people prospered through better methods of trading and fishing, and the children grew chubby and healthy.

By the early 1920's, two hundred baptised believers and many enquirers were meeting regularly for worship and instruction. They were supporting Abasi Mfon and his wife and family and running both Sunday and day schools. Best of all, they were sharing their blessings, for it was Okorotip Christians on fishing expeditions who first carried the Good News to the people of Iko.

One day a deputation of young men presented themselves at Ibuno.

'Where do you come from?' enquired Etubom Bill.

'From Iko, a fishing place near Opobo,' they replied. 'We have listened to the fisherfolk from Okorotip and they tell us good things. We would like somebody to teach us God's fashion also.'

Requests for teachers were pouring in at that time, and suitable men were few. However Iko was too far away to be served by the rota operating from Ibuno, so a promising young man had been sent to live there and was now seeing the fruit of his labours.

As Sam and Gracie Bill sat around the Lord's table with fifty-four communicant members of the little church, their hearts were full of praise and adoration. Back in 1902, when feeling their separation so keenly, Sam had written to a friend – 'Isn't it a great mercy that God has so made us that we can comform to circumstances and limitations when we believe they are imposed by Him?'

Intervening years had tested this spirit of acceptance. Instead of the personal outreach envisaged with the coming of 'Evangel', he had been tied to base by Grace's continuing ill-health and the needs of a growing Mission. All the while, however, the Word was being propagated through national believers, and Iko provided convincing proof of the effectiveness of their witness.

Returning next day to face the demands of a smallpox epidemic at Nditea, the Bills were content. This was where God had placed them and even the limitations were part of His Plan.

CHAPTER FIFTEEN

Compensations

'*There is no man that hath left . . . for My Sake and the gospels, but he shall receive an hundredfold . . .*' *Mark 10:29–30.*

Post-war years are never easy. In Nigeria the early 1920's brought poor prices, and shortage of many basic commodities. Congregations found it difficult to support their preachers and teachers. New sects flooded the area with a spurious Christianity, offering a veneer of respectability with no vital change of heart or life. Some churches, glad of less demanding standards, were attracted away from the Qua Iboe fellowship. In others, ambitious men usurped positions of leadership, keen to be served rather than to serve.

Samuel Bill's report for 1924 referred to 'great struggle and scarcity such as I never knew since I came to Ibuno. Much of our work is like the well-designed and perfectly-finished engine which is useless for anything until supplied with the necessary power. All our carefully-built organisations are futile for doing God's work without the Life-giving Spirit and we feel more and more that this is what we need. There are bright spots, however, and many are earnestly waiting on God. A band of faithful women meet two mornings each week at 5.30 o'clock, seeking God's blessing. Such are the Lord's remembrancers and their prayers will prevail.'

Among the 'bright spots' were Adiaha Ibok, a former

wife of Chief Egbo Egbo, and their daughter Ndarake, who had been one of the Bills' house-girls. In the early months of that year Grace Bill's asthma was exceedingly troublesome.

'I would have frightened you to look at,' she wrote home. 'I just seemed to be dying by inches. Adiaha Ibok came up one day to see me. She said, "I cannot understand it, after all the prayers. Everybody in Ibuno, big and little, in trouble about you and praying for you".

'Then she felt my bones and said, "There is nothing of you left; perhaps God is going to allow you to live till your daughter comes back, and then take you Home" – and she did not mean Ireland!

'Adiaha, and her daughter Ndarake, have had a heavy trial. There were some very fierce tornados this season, and one Friday night the lightning was worse than anyone could remember. Ndarake and her three children were in bed, and she woke up feeling as if her back was burnt. She roused Jessie and told her to waken May, a lovely little thing of five and the only strong child Ndarake has, but wee May had been killed instantly by the flash that struck her mother. She was next to the wall and must have got the full force of it.

'When Ndarake saw what had happened she rushed out through the darkness and torrents of rain and hammered on David's house, crying "Man of God, man of God, get up and get down on your knees before God and ask Him to send the life back into my child".

'She was in an awful state, and went away wringing her hands and saying "Oh God, what sin have I done that You should kill my child". Before morning came, however, she went to her mother with the dead child in her arms and said, "Lord, I see Thy hand. This would not have happened if it had not been Thy Will".

'This was a mighty triumph, for you know how hard it is for people to get away from the thought of witchcraft when they are in sore trouble. There was not a mark on the house or on May's body, but there was a smell of sulphur from her nostrils, from which blood flowed afterwards.

'Poor Ndarake, her troubles are almost more than she can bear; her eldest girl, now thirteen, is nearly blind and has to be led about after dark. I don't think there is a truer Christian in Ibuno than she – and there are some good women there.'

The women of Ibuno church were essentially practical in their witness. It was they who administered the 'Poor Fund' for the relief of widows, and others suffering hardship. They visited the sick, and 'gossipped the gospel' in the compounds of the town and outlying villages. Above all they prayed. Wet or fine, without the customary ringing of the church bell, more than a dozen of them turned up in time for their early morning tryst with God. At their request the Pastor kept a record of their petitions, noting the date of every answer.

'These women are beginning to know what a blessed thing it is to be God's Remembrancers,' he wrote. 'Our blessed Lord is proving to them that He is a prayer-hearing God, by repeated answers which they have received to their prayers. Over a hundred have come with needs to be prayed for, and there is great joy when they report an answer.'

One of the most faithful intercessors was Etia, first convert and first bible-woman of the Qua Iboe Church. When the going had been hard at Okat she went to help the Bailies there, and her quiet, loving ministry had broken down strong opposition and heralded a new day for the women of that area – especially the many twin mothers whom she rescued, with their babies, from banishment and death. Now she was continuing her work at Ibuno and often visited Mrs. Bill's sick-room to bring the latest news and cheer the invalid with her direct and trustful prayers.

'Lord,' she would reason, 'We want Mma to be able to finish the work you sent her here to do, not to see her the way she is. You made her hear Your words "Thou shalt love Thy neighbour as thyself" and with that she cleft a path through the sea and came to open our eyes . . .'

So the prayer would go on, thanking God for all that Grace had been to her in her early Christian life and claiming His healing power. Then, turning to the other women in the room, she reminded them of the four who brought their friend to Jesus. Mrs. Bill never forgot her graphic description of the rustling as they lifted the roof, and the wonderful moment when the Master looked up – 'Those eyes of compassion, those eyes of purity – those lovely eyes looked and *saw their faith.*'

The same compassionate Lord saw the faith of the women of Ibuno. Not only did He spare Mma to them for another eight years, but gave her better health than she had known for a long time.

Grace had been trying to persuade her husband that furlough was overdue, but as usual he had protested, 'It's a waste of the Lord's money and my time.'

The 'going home palaver' as he called it, would begin with a hint that old friends were asking when they would see him again. Then a possible date would be suggested, to fit in with other missionaries who might relieve him of his duties. The factor that usually tipped the scale was Gracie's health and her need for his company on the voyage. But not this time.

'So "himself" has promised to come home next year (D.V.)!!' she wrote to Mac. 'I'm afraid I am like Asquith, and will wait and see!! I had hoped we should get this year, but he does not want to go, and has made it impossible by ordering 100 barrels of cement! It's not *all* love for the work; it's fear of the cold, the hatred of conventionality and of the voyage – and an elderly person's dislike for trouble and change! All the same, I believe the change home would do him good and give him a new outlook. He is wonderfully well, thank God, and has got very stout. His energy and strength are wonderful after $37\frac{1}{2}$ years in Africa.'

Grace Bill knew her man. She could never forget the episode of the drawing-room meeting on a previous furlough. She was to have addressed the ladies, but became ill. Their kindly hostess kept her in bed, persuading the reluctant Sam to deputise. As the room filled up with fashionable hats, and polite conversation, his panic grew. Upstairs he fled and burst unceremoniously into the bedroom, beseeching – 'Gracie, for pity's sake come down and save me!' And, of course, she did.

All the same, even he had to give in eventually. By May 1926, his stock of excuses, and cement, was exhausted. The farewells began on Saturday evening in the home of David and Mary Ekong – who killed a goat in honour of their friends and prepared a delicious meal with all their favourite African dishes. At table with them sat the Ekong's three-year-old granddaughter, doing credit to the training of her grandparents from whom she refused to be separated.

Sunday brought a constant stream of visitors, but Monday was the crowning day. Early in the morning the schoolmaster arrived:

'Etubom,' he announced, 'The school band wishes to play you and Mma down to the beach.'

At three o'clock the procession appeared, school children marching two by two, waving little flags made with white handkerchiefs fastened to sticks, and preceded by two small girls carrying big bunches of flowers in jam pots. Outside the house they halted while the band played. Inside, crowds of well-wishers in Sunday-best cloth embraced their friends, beseeching them to return soon, until eventually David had to hustle them out. On the way to the beach a tiny naked toddler threw his arms around Gracie, and held her tight.

'Eka Kprukpru Ndito!' exclaimed the women – 'the mother of all the children!'

'Three cheers for our manager!' called the school-master. 'And two cheers for Mma!'

These were raised with great gusto and, to the strains of 'God be with you till we meet again,' the Ibuno pastors and elders helped the Bills into the canoe. All around gave last minute exhortations—

'Go – come.'

'Do not forget to return.'

'Don't be afraid,' reassured Gracie. 'We will come back soon.'

The moving scene, so vividly imprinted on her memory, was later described in the Mission magazine:

'... the glorious sunshine, the gay throng, so nicely clothed, the love on the people's faces, the beautiful church in the background ... Thoughts went back 39 years to the first landing of the one they were seeking to honour and one's heart filled with praise to Him "Who has wrought great things for us whereof we are glad".

'When we got on the launch and the engine was started, Mr. Bill went out to wave a final farewell. I shall never forget the audible sigh of love that went up from them all. They remained on the beach till we were a good distance up the river.

' "And no man hath left ... but shall receive in this world an hundredfold!" The severing of home ties is hard – and perhaps gets harder as age creeps on – but the recompense is rich and sure.'

CHAPTER SIXTEEN

The Promised Power

'Ye shall receive power...and ye shall be witnesses unto Me.' Acts 1:8.

'All around is parched and withered. The great heat is sapping all our life and energy. We feel this is an index of the state of the Church here at the present time. As we visit the people, listen to their conversation, go from communion centre to communion centre, the thought is borne in upon us that we need the touch of the Living Spirit of God; and nothing else can serve us.'

Several years passed, after Samuel Bill expressed this conviction, before the spiritual drought was broken in Qua Iboe. He and Grace were not long back from furlough when they heard the first reports of strange happenings at Uyo. No one knew just how the awakening started. Here and there, early morning prayer meetings began to swell and take on new urgency. A solitary Christian at prayer was prostrated by an overwhelming sense of the presence of God. Sharing his experience with fellow teachers, they too were drawn into a blissful fellowship. The message passed from one to another, that in reading the Scriptures, and in prayer and meditation, the power of the life-giving Spirit could be realised by ordinary people.

Missionaries watched and waited, longing for a deep work of the Holy Ghost, yet wary of arousing superficial emotion. As they prayed, conviction of sin intensified. Debts were paid, wrongs righted and broken relationships restored. The course of the movement could not be predicted or directed, but premeditated resistance seemed to prevent any work of grace.

'These were strange days,' wrote the district missionary. 'Days when order and time tables were very much upset. Our cook was greatly used of God and we in no way restrained his activities. He was visited and consulted by scores of enquirers, and often called away into the town. It was greatly to his credit that he very rarely neglected his cooking, and was thoughtful and conscientious in all his work.'

As soon as they could leave Nditia the Bills decided to visit Uyo, and see for themselves what was going on. On the second evening Evangelist Jonathan conducted the service. He started to tell about events at his out-station, where two or three meetings were taking place daily. As he spoke a head man of Idiong secret society entered the church. Walking up to the front he began to speak.

'I have been a thief and an adulterer from my youth,' he confessed brokenly. 'I have killed men in many towns with medicine, and was paid for doing it. I have sought to idols and evil spirits all my life. Now I know they cannot help me. Can your God help me and forgive my sins?'

'There is no other name by which we can be saved, but the name of Jesus,' replied Jonathan, and explained God's willingness to pardon.

'My children are all heathen and they will be very angry with me; my old friends will also be vexed for what I said here tonight. Has your God any word of comfort?'

Opening his Bible at Isaiah 54, Jonathan read:

'Thy children shall all be taught of God ... Thou

shalt not fear . . . no weapon that is formed against thee shall prosper.'

The Idiong man seemed to be reassured by this promise, and went away happy.

'The presence of the Spirit in our meeting was very marked while Jonathan spoke' observed Gracie Bill. 'I rose and started to sing "Let us with a gladsome mind". It was good to hear how they sang it. Many confessed sin and were prayed for, or prayed themselves. One felt it good to be there.

'At the close any who were in trouble were invited to come to the mission house, and two men came, seeking salvation. It was nearly 1 a.m. before we got to rest.

'One of these men spoke in the church next morning, confessing secret sins that he certainly would not have acknowledged apart from the Spirit's work. He was afraid, and had kept away from the meetings till that night.'

In between meetings the Bills heard more about the awakening. Once the missionaries had been roused at midnight by the ringing of the church bell. Getting up to investigate they saw bush lamps coming from all directions through the darkness, and converging on the church

'They had already started praying when I got there,' recalled Jim Westgarth. 'I've never seen a prayer meeting like it. Some were kneeling, some prostrate on their faces. Without leader, or ceremony, each prayed in his own way, with an uprising flood of supplication.'

'Did it get out of hand?' enquired Samuel Bill.

'No. I took no part, and they seemed to take no notice of me, but when prayer had spent itself they turned and asked me to close. As quietly as they had come, they dispersed again to their homes.'

An old man accused several Christians of burning his ju-jus and when they protested that it was at his request, he had them committed to prison. Each night they were bound, but although their hands were secured in different ways, on three successive mornings the handcuffs were off. They claimed that as they sang and praised God light filled the prison and the shackles fell off. The prison warders and District Officer could offer no other explanation of the phenomenon. A few days later the old man asked for their release, confessed to perjury, and entered his name in the enquirers' class to prepare for Christian baptism.

With minds full of what they had seen and heard the Bills returned, 'Hoping and praying the blessing will spread all over the Mission.'

This did not happen. In after years there would be much heart-searching as to whether more might have been done to guide and encourage the movement, but those at the centre of it were sure of one thing – 'As a Mission we should accept it as a token that God is with us. He has put a seal to our labours by bringing to birth a living, spiritual Church.'

The prayer of one quiet man of strong personality and influence, threw a flood of light on the transformation that had taken place: 'Lord, we thought this new religion was man's wisdom, but Thou hast visited us Thyself and we thank and praise Thee.'

The emotion of those memorable days died down, but many future leaders of the Qua Iboe Church traced their spiritual power to the 1928 revival. Years afterwards a visitor asked one evangelist what impression it had left upon him. Burying his face in his hands, he replied, 'Oh, Etubom, it was wonderful! It was WONDERFUL! The Word of God was so sweet; and prayer was our very life.'

Every genuine awakening in the Church's history has issued in missionary outreach, and that in Qua Iboe was no exception. If this was God's message for Africa, then every African should hear it. Sensing the upsurge, the Mission began to investigate possible new fields in the Cameroons, French West Africa, and Igala, two hundred and fifty miles north in Nigeria.

In August 1930 the first Qua Iboe Church conference was held at Ibuno. The church people, always hospitable, were happy to make room in their homes for delegates from different tribal areas, once bitter enemies but now united in Christ Jesus.

One young man could ill afford to feed two extra mouths, but he loved the Lord Jesus and wanted to help. On the morning before Conference he went out fishing. Catches had been so poor lately that there seemed small hope of success. He was drenched with rain as he sat in his canoe but that afternoon he appeared with beaming face at the mission house where Grace Bill was preparing for her guests.

'Mma, it was wonderful!' he exclaimed. 'In a shorter time than ever before I got a larger catch than ever before! God did it and I praise Him.'

Next day the delegates arrived – one hundred and thirty of them, through the worst downpour of the entire season. Earnest prayer had preceded the conference, and from the outset the fellowship was warm and true. It was Mma Etia who welcomed the visitors to Ibuno.

'I thank my God for sparing me to see His children from other places gathering together in the mother church,' she said. 'The Word of God that first came to Ibuno, has spread slowly, slowly, from the river's mouth right up to its source in Ibo country. Farther north there are other places and other people who still do not know the good news. We must not keep it to ourselves.'

Other speakers took up this theme:

'When the missionary first came to our town we reproached him for being so long,' said one. 'Now we must not have other people saying to us "Why did you not bring us this news sooner?" '

Speaking on 'The work of an evangelist' Pastor Jimmy Udo Ema of Etinan district continued: 'You see this beautiful building in which we meet! Why is it here? Because a number of God's people have built it. Why did they build it? Because they turned from idols to worship God. Because Mr. Bill did not say to himself long ago, "I'm glad I'm a Christian. I'm glad I can join with others in Christian work and worship in beautiful buildings in the homeland. I'll stay where I am, happy and comfortable!"

'Had he done so these people would not have received the Gospel. Like Abraham, he heard God's call and went out, not knowing whither he went, but knowing only that God had called him. God wants us, in our turn, to go forth and carry the Good News to others.'

Sam and Grace Bill waited prayerfully to see how Qua Iboe Christians would respond to the need of unknown tribes, with language and customs different to their own. They were not disappointed, for generous gifts and offers of service began to pour in. One young evangelist described his call: 'As Mr. O'Neill told the conference about the people of Igala, and the fact that they did not know anything about our loving Saviour, a sharp feeling came into my mind to follow him into that place. I returned to my station to carry on the work, but the feeling is beating more and more, that I should go and tell them about Christ who died for their sins.'

The Qua Iboe Church, empowered by the life-giving Spirit, had been caught up into the on-going plan of God for the evangelisation of the world.

CHAPTER SEVENTEEN

To Comfort Always

'God ... Who comforteth us that we may be able to comfort them that are in any trouble.' 2 Cor. 1:3–4.

'Etubom, God must have given you a special kind of nose.'

Sam Bill straightened his back and looked at the faces peering in through the dispensary window.

'Why?' he asked.

'Because nobody with an ordinary nose could go near that boy's feet.'

After repeated requests, the mission house had been moved, bit by bit, from Nditea back down to Ibuno. It had been a massive job, but the Bills were delighted to be there again, and the people's pleasure knew no bounds. Their pastor expressed it in one of his regular letters to Mr. McKeown: 'I am pleased to say that the Lord Jesus is still with us. The work is growing, but there is no task added without His help to perform it. You may be sure it is a pleasant sight to us to see Mr. and Mrs. Bill back at Ibuno. The new house is going up on the old site near the spot where the first souls were saved in this land. We pray the Lord will grant His dear servants health to continue to guide the work for many years to come.'

Grace Bill had been dreading the upheaval, but was now full of praise. 'God has done great things for me' she wrote. 'It seems like a miracle the way He has restored my health, enabling me to pack and work, sometimes for hours on end.'

Soon after their arrival they noticed a little fellow, about twelve years old, sitting at the foot of the stairs. He was lame. Indeed he could make no attempt to walk but pulled himself along by heels and hands. His father was dead. His mother, formerly a slave, was too poor and sickly to support her son, and he came to beg for food, or money to buy it in the market.

The trouble in his feet had been caused by chiggers. If these parasites had been dug out in time all would have been well, but the sores festered, the toes rotted away, and each foot became a mass of foul flesh.

When the Ibuno Christians came to preach in the yard where the boy lived, he listened attentively, and hope was born in his heart. Next Tuesday he shuffled along to the church, where the enquirers' class was about to begin.

'Pastor, please put my name on your roll,' he begged. 'I want to be prepared for that country where there is no more hunger or pain.'

David Ekong gave the lad a kindly welcome, but where could he put him? No one could bear to sit near those loathsome feet. The boy did not need to be told. He knew it only too well.

'Pastor,' he offered, 'I will sit outside the door and listen.'

Listen he did, and when the time came for examination he was able to answer all the elders' questions and give a clearer testimony than any other candidate. On the baptismal morning he was brought to the service by one of the elders, while his mother waited to carry him home again on her back.

Then one day he appeared at the dispensary door:
'Etubom, can you do anything for my feet?'

Now Samuel Bill had no special nose, but he could never turn from anyone in need.

'If you come regularly and are very brave I'll see what I can do,' he promised.

So, every morning, the sickly mother carried her son to the dispensary. Every morning other patients scattered, holding their noses. Every morning there were screams of pain as the sores were cleaned and dressed. But mother, son, and missionary persevered until the pain began to ease, the stench lessened and the sores grew smaller.

It was almost four months before healing was complete. True, the feet would never be more than stumps, but they were clean, and no longer painful or offensive to his companions. The boy's joy was great. He still shuffled from the town to the mission house but now he need not stay at the foot of the stairs. Up he scrambled, along the verandah and into the hall to sit on the floor, or at the table with the other children, looking at picture books and playing games. He learned to do simple raffia work, making table baskets and plate mats.

'He was here today, a very happy boy,' wrote Samuel Bill some time later. 'We measured him for a pair of crutches, hoping that when these are made he may be able to get about more comfortably and with more speed; and also he may learn some additional ways of helping to earn his living.'

When Mr. Bill compiled the annual report for Ibuno that year his medical duties were dismissed in the customary few words – 'As usual we had a busy time in the little hospital and dispensary, where our work is much appreciated, thousands of patients being treated.'

Conditions were changing in West Africa. Government doctors were being sent out, and new regulations were expected to restrict the activities of non-qualified practitioners. This was good and necessary, but in practice Mr. Bill knew it could mean that people near the Government centres would be catered for, and inaccessible places like Ibuno deprived of the meagre facilities they now enjoyed. What Qua Iboe needed was its own doctor and mission hospital, to supervise and supplement the local dispensaries. Once he had looked forward to his own son heading up the medical team, but Jack was gone. For a long time prayers for a doctor remained unanswered.

It was 1926 when Dr. Bernard Wheatley joined the Mission, of which his brother was already a member That year an excellent site was obtained at Etinan, overlooking the river and a broad vista of palm forest. On January 4 1928 Samuel Bill dedicated the new hospital to the service and glory of God.

'Wherever the Gospel is carried,' he said in his address, 'two things are always linked together, preaching, and healing. Christ chose the twelve and gave them power to heal. The doctor may have skill, yet the power of God is necessary for healing of both body and soul. This fine hospital is an expression of the love and obedience of God's people who have built and equipped it out of love to Christ. It is also a witness to the fact that God answers prayer.'

Mr. Bill went on to speak of patients known to him who had died for lack of hospital facilities, and of two who had been seriously ill for many years and been cured already through the doctor's skill.

A fellow missionary commented afterwards: 'I felt some tribute should have been paid to the many lives he had saved before we had a doctor or hospital on the field. I remember one case myself. A man was brought to the mission house at midnight. He had been dreadfully wounded in a fight after a heathen play. His face was cut open from the right side of his forehead to the left of his chin. It took fifteen stitches to close the wound. He got quite well except that he lost an eye, and he is now a Christian. Many of his friends said he was more beautiful after his operation!'

After a couple of years Dr. Wheatley had to return home because of his wife's ill-health, but before leaving, he had been joined by Dr. Charlie Ross, who was destined to take a son's place in the hearts of Sam and Grace Bill. He it was who taught Mr. Bill to give injections, and supplied him with a drug which acted like magic against the old enemies, yaws and ulcers. The fame of these injections spread like wildfire. People came in crowds to be 'kimmed' ('pricked'). It was wonderful to have a hospital within reach, but the Bills still had more than enough to do – as Sam's report for the year reflected: 'One feature is the marked increase in the work of the dispensary – to such an extent that Mrs. Bill's strength, and my own, are taxed to the utmost.'

The same report began with a sad reference to one whom medical skill had been unable to cure: 'The death of Pastor David Ekong on 17 March plunged the towns and churches in the whole district into deep sorrow.'

It was while conducting gospel meetings in one of the newer churches that David Ekong became ill. 'Behold I come quickly' had been his text that Sunday morning when he told over eight hundred people in his congregation: 'If the Lord comes and takes me Home from Ikot Idong I shall be looking around, watching to see if you all arrive safely in Heaven.'

His closing prayer encompassed everyone and everything about the town. It almost seemed as if he could not stop praying. Shortly afterwards he developed a high fever, followed by paralysis. When it became clear that nothing further could be done for him in hospital, he was moved home to Ibuno, where his wife and Mr. and Mrs. Bill were constantly at his bedside.

'I am looking to the glory that is coming,' he assured them, before slowly sinking into unconsciousness.

'I stayed with him till the end – just before the second bell began to ring,' wrote Samuel Bill. 'He passed away without regaining consciousness. There is not a sound in Ibuno today.'

On any count David Ekong was a great man. In 1924 a British government official published a book entitled 'Life in Southern Nigeria' in which he stated: 'Practically the whole Ibuno tribe has now been converted to Christianity through the efforts of the Qua Iboe Mission under the leadership of Mr. Bill . . . Mr. David Ekong – the native minister, eldest son of the ruling family . . . is a man of considerable intelligence. His superior learning, combined with the prestige of his birth, has secured for him great influence among the tribe . . .'

The deepest secret of Pastor David's influence, however, did not lie in position or education – advantages which might have made a lesser man proud, and alienated him from his own people.

From his early conversion, the personal life of the chief's son had been exposed to close and constant scrutiny. Watching his reaction to persecution, to the loss of dearly-loved children, to the prolonged illness of his wife, and, in later years, to false and bitter accusations, the Ibunos had come to respect their pastor first and foremost as a man of God. His passionate sermons, his clear exposition of truth, his convincing pamphlets on such sensitive subjects as polygamy and strong drink, his wise advice, and words of comfort – all these bore the marks of God-given authority. In the strangely silent hours following his death, and for many years to come, these were the things by which he was remembered.

A few months previously, in a letter acknowledging receipt of an old photograph, Pastor David had unwittingly summed up his own life story, since that night when he first learned the secret of abiding in Christ:

'The sight of my photo when I was a boy of fifteen years old has brought back to me what I was at the time when the Lord took hold of me and would not let me serve the devil. I can say, as Samuel of old, "Hitherto has the Lord helped me" . . . For these forty years there has not been a break between me and my Lord Jesus.'

During those forty years, in the Plan of God, David Ekong and Samuel Bill had worked together with unbroken harmony and mutual enrichment. It was fitting that the end of their earthly partnership found them, hand in hand, within sound of Ibuno church bell.

CHAPTER EIGHTEEN

Across the River

'When thou passest ... through the rivers they shall not overflow thee.' Isaiah 43:2.

The doctor's house at Etinan hospital was always a hospitable place. On May 17 1932 the sound of animated conversation and laughter issued from doors and windows, as eighteen missionaries and four children caught up on each other's news, and enjoyed the delicacies prepared for a very special occasion. Grace Bill was sixty-five years old that day, and the surprise party had been planned in her honour.

Seven months earlier Dr. Ross had been summoned to Ibuno where Mrs. Bill lay, tossing with high fever and severe abdominal pain. His diagnosis was predictable. Nothing could be done for the suspected tumour, but she would probably get over this acute phase and have a few more months among them. There followed a period of extreme suffering, which the combined efforts of doctor, nurses, devoted husband and daughter could do little to alleviate. Seeing no possibility of healing they felt compelled to share her desire for a speedy release, but at the same time Ibuno Christians were praying day and night for her recovery.

'It must be very hard for the Lord to know what to do with all these prayers!' commented one of her nurses.

One evening when the end seemed near, Grace suddenly began to improve. No one could account for the dramatic change, but, slowly and steadily, a measure of strength was regained. The next mail brought a letter from R. L. McKeown, telling how at the end of a Council meeting, members had felt constrained to linger for prolonged prayer. God had drawn unusually near and all went away convinced that their supplication had been heard and answered. Could the Bills recall any special need at that time? It proved to be the very day and hour when Gracie began to recover.

By December she was sitting up in bed, preparing the church books for end-of-year audit. By February the doctor reckoned she was fit to travel to Etinan. Under his daily supervision she made further progress, and, by May, was getting ready to return to Ibuno. Her birthday coincided with executive meetings and this seemed an ideal time to gather the mission family around the frail little lady whom they look upon as a mother.

It would be impossible to assess the influence of Grace Bill upon the Qua Iboe Mission and Church Though never physically robust, she was strong in faith, fervent in spirit and clear in vision. A far more eloquent speaker than her husband, her challenging words had been used of God to call many into His service, and her unswerving dedication held them to the highest. In answer to prayer she had been granted a few more months among them, and they wanted her to feel the support and warmth of their love. It was a highly successful birthday party, deeply appreciated by both Samuel and Grace Bill.

Next day they set out for Ibuno. The weather was cruelly hot, and many visitors awaited their arrival, but by nightfall Mr. Bill could record thankfully: 'She is now safely in bed, and not too tired.'

The respite was short lived. Intense heat and a series of boils soon sapped the meagre store of strength. Grace was urged to go home to Ireland, but felt unfit to travel.

Besides, she knew the end was near and it was her deep desire to die in Africa and await the resurrection there among her friends.

By July one lung was congested and she was fighting for breath. Her husband's heart grew heavy with the inevitability of coming parting, and although the Ibuno Christians still kept their vigil of prayer, they too knew they could not hold her much longer.

For two days before the end she was mercifully free from pain. Then on August 12, fully conscious and with Etia, now nearly ninety years of age, among the loved ones at her bedside, Grace Bill entered into the joy of her Lord. As David Ekong's successor, Pastor William Usen, put it – 'Many a time Mma Bill has waited for the boat to ferry her across the river! Now Christ has come to fetch her. How happy she was to embark with Him for the other side!'

Even in his personal grief, Samuel Bill's first thought was for the people. Hundreds of them streamed quietly up the stairway, gazed with tear-filled eyes at the worn but lovely face, and made their way out again along the paths she had often travelled to bring comfort in their sorrows. They would never forget Mma's love.

On the evening of the funeral, Mr. Bill sat down to write his diary:

'This has been a memorable day. We laid dear Gracie to rest behind the church – not where I had first thought, at the side of the house here. I did this because the people seemed to wish it ... The church was packed, and many were outside. Representatives took part from all parts of the field. Big Town and our own choir sang in the house before the coffin was lifted and all joined in singing Psalm 90. Many beautiful wreaths were made, and laid on the grave ... Everyone has shown sympathy and love.'

"......... the frail little lady........"

Next day Samuel Bill got up as usual to attend to his patients. Some were waiting for injections, which he administered as in a daze. Suddenly, he felt sick and dizzy and had to retire to bed. He was due to leave with Emma in the morning, and with an effort, was able to do so, feeling better when he got to Mbiuto, where Emma now lived with her missionary husband, John McClements.

It was September 11 before he had to face up to living alone – almost forty-six years since, aboard the steamer for Calabar, he had been wondering how his bride-to-be would react to Africa.

'The thought often strikes me,' read his diary entry for September 30 1887, 'what will Gracie think of the people, when she sees them, and how will she like to live among them? And my heart always answers that that will be all right, for the God Who has helped us, and opened up our way hitherto, will be with us in this, and cause us to rejoice in His blessed work.'

Sam Bill's heart had not misled him. Now a fresh challenge lay ahead.

'This evening I feel as if I were on the eve of a new experience and a new life,' he wrote, on his first night back at Ibuno. 'From tomorrow I shall be alone – no one to talk to and tell every little thing, but I suppose I shall get used to it.'

The strangest element in his loneliness was that for the first time he could not record the day's happenings, and post the letter off to Grace. Only the fresh mound of earth alongside David's grave kept reminding him that she was not in Belfast, but in the heavenly Homeland.

God's comfort came in many different guises. On the evening of the day Grace died, a small figure slipped unobtrusively into the house. When bedtime came she was still there with the house-girls. Etubom did not need to be told that David Ekong's little granddaughter meant to stay and keep him company.

The pastors and elders were concerned about him too. They wrote direct to the Mission Council: 'Mrs. Bill, who was to us everything, and whom both you and ourselves had wished God would spare . . . is no longer in our midst. When Etubom first came out to Qua Iboe he was then a young man, with little or no need of a helper. But now, the state in which he is, his true and faithful helper taken away . . . we earnestly entreat you to consider this petition of ours – that a man be set apart to help the work in Ibuno district.'

Perhaps, somewhere, a young man heard the call of God, as had Samuel Bill forty-five years before. If so, he allowed it to be stiffled, for no new helper came.

One sleepless night, after a day which had brought vivid reminders of Grace, her husband thought how pleasant it would be if Emma could live with him. But the McClements were fully occupied in their own work at Mbiuto. It would be selfish to expect them to move. Besides, they were soon due for furlough and the last thing he wanted to do was to accompany them. So, while she was available, Emma came for a week each month to Ibuno, and when his work took him up-country her father spent a few days at her home. Other missionaries too, made a point of visiting when they could find time for a family outing, a weekend, or a quick call to make sure all was well. And the Ibunos were always there, watchful and considerate.

Samuel Bill's seventieth birthday found him at Etinan for the annual conference. Painful boils on his neck prevented him from attending some of the meetings. They did not, however, deter him from inspecting the leprosy settlement recently established nearby, under the supervision of a new missionary, Donald Currie. 'The right man for the job,' was his verdict.

As President of the Mission, Mr. Bill was now leaving the main burden of administration to younger men on Field Executive. The title 'elder statesman' might not have appealed to him, but a remarkable blend of homely wisdom, hard-won experience and spiritual insight fitted him to probe unerringly to the heart of problems, which multiplied with passing years. He would sit tapping the arm of his chair and listening intently while every view-point was presented. Then, when he thought discussion had gone on long enough, he would quietly intervene with what usually proved to be the conclusive word. He did not like to be rushed into any decision. 'I want to order my thoughts according to the Lord's mind, feeling well assured that there is no success along any other line,' he had written long ago to the Mission's secretary. Or, as he put it characteristically in his diary – 'You can't always hit the nail on the head on the spur of the moment!'

In October 1933, news came from Etinan of the sudden death of Pastor Jimmy Udo Ema, John Kirk's first houseboy, whom Samuel Bill described as a man of 'sterling character – strong and straight.' Seated beside the widow at the funeral in a packed church, Mr. Bill's thoughts were far away.

'I was wondering, all the time of the service what Jimmy and David and Mr. Kirk and Gracie were doing up Above,' he recorded that night.

Heaven seemed strangely near these days and as the books were prepared for the end of the year he asked himself, 'Shall I see another audit?' The question spurred him on to making provision, in the event of his death, for the support of Abita, his faithful dispensary helper, whose wife had just given birth to a baby girl—

named Grace. Everything must be in order when the Call came.

This mood soon passed, however, when John and Emma returned from furlough looking rested and well. 'I am delighted to have them back,' he acknowledged. 'It means contentment to me to have them here.'

Early in 1934 the three of them set off on a very special journey. Northwards they sped, in John McClements' Sunbeam car, along a good road which led through palm forest to open hilly country. They camped overnight in a government rest house and next day reached Adoru, the most southerly of the Mission's Igala stations. That evening Mr. Bill addressed a little prayer meeting, before leaving again for Gwalawo:

'The work of all the places seems very promising. We are very glad to have seen it. But,' he admitted 'the travelling is very tiring to one of my age.'

Nevertheless, before the year was out Samuel Bill was back in Igala, accompanying the general secretary on a fact-finding tour of the new fields. It was encouraging to note the progress of the past ten months. In answer to many prayers a site had been granted in the strategic principal town of Idah. Across the river Benue, a foothold had been obtained and an interpreter miraculously provided for outreach to the neglected Bassa people. But the highlight of the visit was the baptism of the first sixteen Igala believers, followed by a Communion service in the little grass-roofed church at Gwalawo.

'A moving experience,' was the comment of a young missionary who was present to hear the message given by the ageing pioneer.

On their return journey, Mr. Bill and Mr. McKeown stayed at one of the two flourishing mission centres in the vast Ibo tribe, which had once seemed so remote and inaccessible. In those early days Sam Bill had asked for two hundred souls to be led into the Kingdom of Jesus Christ before his life-work ended. Now, forty-seven years later, he was seeing the answer – multiplied two hundredfold.

CHAPTER NINETEEN

Master Builder

'The grace of God ... given unto me, as a wise Master Builder.' I Cor. 3:10

The policeman on point duty at a busy Belfast road junction blinked his eyes and looked again. Approaching, from the wrong direction down a one-way street, was a small Humber car.

As the car drew near he raised a white-gloved hand and stooped to inspect its occupants. A pair of innocent blue eyes met his own with a disconcertingly direct gaze.

'Good day,' said the driver.

'Where do you think you're going?' demanded the law. 'Don't you know that's a one-way street.'

'I'm sorry,' came the calm reply. 'You see I'm not used to driving in the city.'

The policeman looked with surprise at the elderly gentleman and his two lady passengers, sallow-complexioned and warmly wrapped in heavy tweed coats, that mild June day in 1937.

'Where do you come from anyway?' he pursued.

'West Africa.'

'Hmm. Well, the sooner you get back there the better!'

Samuel Bill couldn't have agreed more. Left to himself, he would never have moved from Ibuno after Gracie's death. But this was the Qua Iboe Mission's fiftieth year. Jubilee meetings demanded the presence of its Founder.

Early in January the celebrations had begun with crowded gatherings in Ibuno Church. Twenty-three white people were there, but this was essentially the Ibunos' day and they made the most of it, uniting to praise God in their beautiful church, on the very spot where their forefathers had offered pagan sacrifice. Afterwards, they made a great feast for their guests, presenting Etubom with an illuminated address and a purse – 'Gratifying but embarrassing'.

It was several days before he received the money, of which the purse was a token. The great pile of coins – many three-pence pieces, pennies and halfpennies – was to Samuel Bill like the water from the well of Bethlehem which David could not drink. On January 13 he travelled to Etinan for the annual conference. One item under discussion was the urgent appeal for a Bible Training Institute, at which pastors and preachers could obtain a higher level of training. Mr. Bill's diary for that evening records – 'I have given the £50 I received as a presentation gift to the B.T.I.'

Etinan, too, had to have its special Jubilee service, with representatives from all over the field. The pioneer delved into his old diaries to get facts and dates right for another survey of early days. There were further presentations, one 'a beautiful chair with cushions.' He couldn't give that away!

More was to follow. On February 11 a deputation of local women arrived at the mission house with their own address and gift. They felt they owed more than anyone else to the coming of the Gospel, and wanted to say 'Thank You' to God and to His servant. 'It was utterly unexpected,' Sam commented. 'The whole thing touched me more deeply than any of the Jubilee happenings.'

On the Sunday before leaving, he preached, significantly, on the text, 'Take heed how ye build.'

The following days were hectically busy. 'A fierce day,' he wrote on April 16. 'Trying to get things put in order for leaving, but many interruptions from people and deputations coming to say goodbye, and consult on all kinds of matters. Had a visit from all the chiefs – very cordial and kind. A hearty goodbye.'

Next morning he was off with Emma on the first stage of their homeward journey. Three weeks later they were welcomed at Belfast dock by John McClements who had travelled earlier because of illness, and a big crowd of council members and friends, photographers and reporters.

The end of June found Mr. Bill at Portstewart for the annual 'Keswick' Convention. It was refreshing to sit under the ministry of good men like Dr. John McBeath, whose quiet, devotional Bible readings ran deep and true. He enjoyed the fun and fellowship in the Qua Iboe Mission house-party and afternoon excursions to beauty spots on the lovely Antrim coast, but those who knew him best detected the far-away look in his eyes as he gazed across the Atlantic breakers.

'It won't be long till I get back to Ibuno now', he'd say, half-fearful lest anything should hinder his return.

On Friday the big tent was filled for the missionary meeting. Under the banner, 'All One in Christ Jesus' missionaries from all parts of the world assembled on the platform. As one of the few Ulster-born and based societies, the Qua Iboe Mission held a unique place in the hearts of 'Portstewart regulars.' Indeed, Convention and Mission shared one gifted secretary in the person of R. L. McKeown. It had taken all his considerable powers of persuasion to get that day's guest of honour on to the platform.

The stocky figure, topped by an unruly quiff of white hair, listened self-consciously to the gracious tributes paid to his fifty years as founder and leader of the Qua Iboe Mission. Embarrassment increased as the vast congregation rose spontaneously to do him honour. There was no escape route through that crowd of missionaries. He would have to reply. He couldn't let Mac down. But what would he say?

Clutching the front rail firmly with one hand, and running the other nervously up and down the upright support of the awning, he stammered, 'Thank you friends for your welcome, but I don't deserve all this fuss. I only did ordinary things, like teaching a few children to read, helping a few sick folk, keeping engines running. It was God who did it all.'

That night, in the privacy of his hotel bedroom he wrote, 'Attended the afternoon missionary meeting in the tent. Felt very much put about at allusions to me – very flattering and made me feel most uncomfortable. However, I am over with it now and shall get to Belfast in the morning D.V.'

It was on his way into the city that he encountered the police but 'although they took my name they said I would hear no more about it.'

Wherever Mr. Bill went his attitude to publicity was the same. He hated the tendency to elevate missionaries on a pedestal. Sometimes his friends, knowing how audiences loved romantic accounts of missionary exploits, wished they could get him talking more freely about the adventures and miracles he had experienced. But that was not his way.

Before returning to Nigeria one more ordeal had to be faced – a 50th anniversary broadcast on the B.B.C. At least he was able to prepare this in advance and read it from a script without an audience of white faces!

As usual there was no elaborating on the darkness of

Africa or the personal cost of missionary service. But he did place on record that the Gospel had spread to six tribes; that 560 churches, and almost as many schools, had on their rolls 43,000 communicant members, and over 12,000 pupils; that there were now 46 missionaries and over 1,000 national workers. Twenty of the latter were being supported by the Qua Iboe Church as evangelists in their northern mission field of Igala and Bassa, and, in the south, 6,400 copies of the Efik Bible had been sold during the past year.

'In a broadcast like this it is impossible to go into details', he concluded, 'but God has wrought a wonderful work.'

Early in November Samuel Bill set sail for the last time aboard S.S. Apapa. It was an unpleasant journey. Before leaving London he had contracted a cold and the weather, at first too chilly, became unbearably hot as they neared Nigeria.

'It completely floored me, and I felt quite unfit for anything for about a month after my arrival,' he wrote in January. 'I have been thinking much of Mrs. Bill the last three days – the reason being that dear old Etia has gone Home . . . The infirmities of age and sickness had her in their grip and she slipped quietly away. My thoughts went with her, to the happy awakening in His presence, Whom she loved; and to those who had gone before her – Egbo, Ibok, David and Mrs. Bill.

That inner circle was keenly missed, later in the year when yet another honour was conferred on the founder of the Mission, this time in the context of the British Empire. He described the event in a letter to a friend: 'I was summoned to Eket the other day (August 31 1938) to meet the Chief Commissioner of Southern Nigeria, who wished to present me with the badge and medal of the M.B.E. The Government folk seemed to regard it as a rather important ceremony. There was a guard of honour, consisting of a white commissioner of police and about seventy policemen, called in from different parts of Nigeria for the occasion, also the District Officers and the Senior Resident from Calabar. They had shelters put up for the visitors and the Government had notified all the missionaries.

'Hundreds of Ibunos were present, and many people from other parts. The Chief Commissioner made a speech – fairly long, giving a rapid sketch of the starting of the Mission and its subsequent growth. I don't know where he got all his facts – some of them would hardly bear investigation! But he went into the matter of the state of the Ibunos in the early days and of their progress in Christianity, education, and many other ways.

'It was very interesting and I, having been assured at the outset that I would not be expected to make a speech, rather enjoyed it. The C.C. at the end pinned the medal on my left breast and a police bugler played something as a finish up, after which there was much hand-shaking. We adjourned to the D.O.'s bungalow for tea or lemonade and some conversation with the officials.'

What Mr. Bill did not describe was the difficulty the organisers had in extricating him from among his Ibuno friends to have tea in the bungalow. The honour was for them to share, and he wanted everybody to see his medal. Besides, he was far happier in their company.

Just 34 years previously Samuel Bill had received an invitation from the High Commissioner to become Political Officer for Qua Iboe District. He would have been proud to serve his country and there was much he might have done in that capacity, for the good of the people he loved – not to mention enjoying a secure and lucrative position. He turned down the offer without a backward look. He had a bigger job in hand and one that would take every ounce of his strength for the whole of his life – as a 'Master Builder' of the Church, planned and purchased to be the dwelling place of its Divine Architect.

CHAPTER TWENTY

One Clear Call

'The time of my departure has come.' 2 Tim. 4:6.

It was a glorious moonlit night, and on the verandah of Ibuno mission house a missionary teacher was pacing to and fro, lost in thought. The peaceful river scene had become very familiar since her first visit in March 1933. How vividly she could recall that memorable introduction!

She had just begun teaching in the Girls' Institute at Afaha Eket, later known as Grace Bill School, when the school manager, accompanied by his daughter, arrived for his fortnightly visit. Her immediate impression of Samuel Bill was of two piercing blue eyes that seemed to search the soul. Maybe those keen eyes, under their bushy brows, detected that the object of their scrutiny was wilting in the unaccustomed heat, and could do with a breath of sea air.

'Come on, Miss Tector', he said. 'Get your helmet and come down to Ibuno.'

The regulation sun helmet and a few other belongings were quickly collected, and before long they were on the way. As the launch glided smoothly through the clear water, Andrew, cook-cum-engineer, served tea with delicious bread of his own baking, tinned salmon, and marmalade. Not a breath stirred the foliage of palm and mangrove trees fringing the river bank. Leaving the girls to entertain each other, Mr. Bill stretched himself on a seat and went fast asleep.

".... pointing heavenwards among the palm fronds...."

Three hours later the river had widened and the breeze freshened. The distant sound of breakers could be heard, and there on the bank stood the famous Ibuno church, its tall steeple pointing heavenwards among the palm-fronds. On the beach several hefty men were waiting. When the launch stopped they waded into the water and, to the visitor's intense surprise, first

Emma, then Etubom, and finally she herself were carried pick-a-back to dry land.

There was plenty to interest a newcomer to Ibuno – the rail truck carrying heavy loads from jetty to workshop; the hospital ward full of patients with many ailments; the spacious, homely house, lit from an electric light plant donated by a Belfast friend, and, delight of delights, the little organ. Samuel Bill quickly discovered that his guest had an auto-harp, and a good singing voice. She, in turn, soon realised that the Mission's founder was as ready to listen to the views of a junior probationer as to those of his most experienced colleagues.

Next morning at breakfast came the usual question,
'Do you like porridge?'

An affirmative answer met with an approving nod and, 'You'll do.' For how could anyone do a decent day's work without a good plate of porridge?

A decent day's work was expected of all comers. They were also expected to take sensible precautions to guard their health.

'You'll never stick this climate if you rush around like that', he'd warn. 'Never run when you can walk, never walk when you can sit, and never sit when you can lie.'

And to set a good example he would stretch out on his favourite bamboo couch.

Another of Mr. Bill's characteristics was his insistence on punctuality. One day Mabel Tector and Emma were relaxing in a canoe on the river when the church bell reminded them that it was six o'clock. Pulling hard for the shore, they scrambled up the bank, dashed along the path and up the stairs. At the dining-table Father Bill sat supping his soup. Not a word was spoken as he looked meaningfully from the breathless girls to the clock on the wall. They were two minutes late. The look and the lesson were not lost on the young teacher, who was soon to prove the need of strict self-discipline for those called upon to discipline others.

Ibuno was only eight miles by land from the Girls' Institute and sometimes Mabel set out by bicycle, accompanied by a boy to help carry the machine across swampy areas while she groped for a footing on submerged logs. The last stretch lay through thick sand and it was a thankful traveller who eventually reached journey's end and a refreshing bath.

After such a trek, one Christmas vacation, Mr. Bill announced at dinner-time: 'I'm doing the school returns for the year and I need some statistics. Can you give them to me?'

'I'm afraid I would have to consult the records' came the hesitant reply.

'Well, I must know as soon as possible, to get my report off by the next mail.'

The teacher's heart sank. There was nothing for it but to return to Afaha Eket. Next morning she set out after breakfast, getting help through the swamp from passers-by, and reaching the school in record time.

Sam Bill was on the verandah when she got back to Ibuno. Indoors the table was being laid for lunch.

'Where have you been?' he enquired.

'At Afaha Eket' replied the weary girl, handing over the required papers.

'Well I never!'

The manager looked at her with growing respect. Then with the familiar twinkle he added, 'Wait till I tell those boys who take the whole day when I send them on an errand. If a slip of a girl can do it between meals, so should they!'

An unexpected treat was in store for the Christmas guests that year. Since her mother's death, Emma had been busy around Ibuno, organising a Christian Endeavour Society and training a choir, among other activities. This year she had taught one of the members to wield the conductor's baton while she accompanied on the organ.

The church was packed for the Christmas morning service. As usual, Father, arrayed in Sunday black, walked sedately from the mission house with his daughter on his arm. He mounted the curved stair to the roomy pulpit, for, although he seldom preached, his presence there seemed to give confidence to the Pastor and satisfaction to the people. Emma took her place at the organ. Jumbo marshalled his choir, and soon the rafters were ringing with rich, vibrant voices blending triumphantly in the Hallelujah Chorus from Handel's 'Messiah'.

These unforgettable memories flooded in upon Mabel Tector as she gazed down the moonlit river, and listened to the rhythmic booming of the breakers. Mingling with them came familiar words that were assuming a new significance:

> 'Sunset and evening star,
>   And one clear call for me!
> And may there be no moaning at the bar,
>   When I put out to sea.'

For, in his room nearby, lay Samuel Bill, semi-paralysed after a cerebral haemorrhage. It was not the first warning of the approaching end of an epoch. In June 1941, writing to sympathise with the McKeown family in the damage sustained to their home and church in the blitz on Belfast, Mr. Bill had said, 'My health is slightly improved. I have just had a slight attack like the first when my speech was again affected for a short time. I don't think I shall go to Conference. I don't feel like it this time . . . I remember you daily in prayer.'

From this stroke, too, he rallied for a time. In December he went for treatment to Port Harcourt, but refused to stay longer than a fortnight because 'the medicine room audit was fully due, and after that the station audit, and it behoved me to get back to look after these things.'

At the time of Thomas Akpan's death Gracie Bill had received a letter from her husband which read: 'If it were God's will I should like to die as Thomas died. You know I don't like to be hurried in getting ready to go any place – but to have plenty of time. So I should like it to be at the last, and so it seemed to be with Thomas. His chariot has been a very peaceful one – and very little pain.'

Forty years later God granted His servant's request. He had plenty of time to get ready, and to hand over his duties one by one. When his call came at 8.35 a.m. on January 24 1942, all was peaceful and serene. His last conscious act had been to beckon a little girl to his bedside and kiss her goodbye – a symbolic farewell to many small ones hovering around in unaccustomed quietness.

When word spread that Etubom had died, the Ibunos took over. He had approved the hymn-singing with which the church people replaced their ancient death wailing. Now as the long procession passed through his room, they sang softly all the psalms and hymns he loved so dearly.

Several missionaries took part in the funeral services but, at Mr. Bill's request, the major portion was in African hands. Pastor Abasi Mfon spoke in the house, and in the church an address was given by Pastor William Usen. Taking as his theme the words of Philip in John 14:8, 'Lord, shew us the Father and it sufficeth us', he recalled the various ways in which Etubom Bill had revealed the Father to the people of Ibuno – by the life he lived, by his wise counsel, guidance and friendship, by his patience and love for little children.

'His house was open to all', he said, 'but his special joy was when the children gathered there on Sunday afternoons to sing hymns and choruses.'

Speaking with deep emotion, Pastor William comforted the weeping people by reminding them that although God had called Etubom Home, He had not left them without His Word, His Holy Spirit and His great love.

After the service, singing 'Safe in the arms of Jesus', the Ibuno Christians reverently laid all that was mortal of Samuel Alexander Bill in the warm earth of his beloved Africa, beside his wife and their two friends, David and Mary Ekong.

Meanwhile, news of the Founder's death had reached Belfast. R. L. McKeown, himself far from well, wrote a moving tribute for the February issue of the Mission magazine, in which he referred to Mr. Bill's great understanding of the African people and his ability, while upholding Scriptural standards in the church, to avoid rigid or mechanical laws. He recalled the pioneer's exceeding modesty, his independence of mind, his physical stamina, his medical skill and practical ingenuity. Then he probed to the most important characteristic of all –

'Although he did not talk easily about the deeper things of the soul, he was a truly spiritual man, with an intimate knowledge of God. To hear him pray was an inspiration. He was like a little child taking his Heavenly Father by the hand and pleading his need before the Throne of Grace.'

Before that tribute could be printed, Mr. McKeown had followed his friend to the Father's House, and the Mission's annual meeting, on March 31, became a memorial service for the two who had been described as 'the men of the knotted hearts.'

In writing of Samuel Bill, R. L. McKeown had expressed what was equally true of himself – 'With his Master, he could say to his heavenly Father, "*I have finished the work that Thou gavest me to do!*" '

Built to Last

'If the work which any man has built on the foundation survives, he will receive a reward.' 1 Cor. 3:14.

Three decades after the death of Samuel Bill, a little group of missionaries' children on a sight-seeing expedition clustered round their teacher as she tried to decipher the names on the weathered headstones beside Ibuno church.

'Auntie, where did Mr Bill live?' asked one youngster.

'Over there,' she replied, indicating a levelled site near the river bank. 'The house became dangerous and had to be pulled down in case of accidents. Look, that's the big water tank. It must have been well made to survive all these years.'

'The church hasn't fallen down,' observed another child thoughtfully.

'No,' agreed the teacher, turning to survey the stout walls and slender spire. 'The church was built to last. Let's go and look inside.'

All was quiet in the cool, dimly lit church. The old brass lamps hung in their brackets. The graceful stair and hand- rail curved up to the wide mahogany pulpit. It was easy to picture Pastor David Ekong preaching there, with Samuel Bill seated beside him.

Out in the sunshine once again the children's mood changed as they raced to the beach to inspect the modern jetty, alive with speed-boats, jeeps and bulldozers. That afternoon, ten miles up-river at Eket, they clambered aboard a helicopter, used to ferry Shell-B.P. personnel to their off-shore oil rig. For Nigeria had struck oil with its precarious prosperity and attendant problems.

If Samuel Bill could have taken an evening stroll on his verandah, as in days gone by, he would have seen that night sky illumined by the distant glow of burning gas. He would have viewed with concern the influence of a cosmopolitan community, as oil-men of many nationalities congregated in places of entertainment undreamed of in his time. One thing is sure; whatever his age, Samuel Bill would have been in his element among the children that day, exploring those new and exciting means of transport. To him every change presented fresh challenge, and every invention was another vehicle to be harnessed for the spread of the Good News.

It is symbolic that although Ibuno Mission House has long since been dismantled, the church still stands. The outbreak of civil strife in 1966 found the Mission in process of handing over the reins of government and leases of property to the Qua Iboe Church, which had been progressively assuming responsibility for all medical, educational and church affairs. Soon the whole area was engulfed in prolonged hostilities which imposed widespread suffering and the temporary withdrawal of missionaries. When fighting eventually ended, the severed sections of the Qua Iboe Church came together for their united conference.

'What will happen?' wondered the returning missionaries. 'Will Ibo and Ibibio members ever be able to work together again?'

Fears were quickly rebuked as leaders greeted each other with tears and joyful embraces.

'We do not need to be reconciled,' they affirmed. 'In Christ we have never been separated.'

The Qua Iboe missionaries had come back in response to urgent appeals for graduate teachers, medical specialists, and theological tutors to assist in training a Bible-based ministry for over eight hundred and fifty congregations. Since then each passing year has seen more well-qualified Nigerians filling these senior positions and the Qua Iboe Church has continued to grow and mature. With the completion of the handover in 1981, the Mission scaffolding finally disappeared, to be replaced by a new Fellowship, and an even deeper relationship of mutual caring and support.

Standing on the threshold of our second century, we are aware of the massive problems and opportunities facing the church of Jesus Christ in Nigeria. Circumstances are very different to those encountered by Samuel Bill and David Ekong, but the plan, the promise and the power of God remain steadfast and utterly reliable – *'I will build My Church and the gates of hell shall not prevail against it.'*